TRANSITION TO A GLOBAL SOCIETY

Professor Suheil Bushrui, an author, poet, critic, translator and broadcaster of international reputation, is currently Distinguished Visiting Fellow and Director of the Gibran Chair on Values and Peace at the Center for International Development and Conflict Management at the University of Maryland.

Iraj Ayman is Director of the Landegg Academy and the Institute of International Education and Development, Wienacht, Switzerland, and consultant to UNESCO. Dr Ayman's international experience covers a wide range of activities including work with international educational and psychological associations.

Ervin Laszlo, member of the Club of Rome, is the Rector of the Vienna Academy and the Director of its Institute for Evolutionary Studies. He is the founder and head of the General Evolution Research Group, Science Adviser to the Director-General of UNESCO, Consultant to the United Nations University and General Secretary of the European Culture Impact Research Consortium. He has published many books and papers and is the Executive Editor of the *World Encyclopedia of Peace*.

transition to a
Global
Society

edited by

SUHEIL BUSHRUI,
IRAJ AYMAN & ERVIN LASZLO

introduction by

FEDERICO MAYOR
DIRECTOR-GENERAL OF UNESCO

ONEWORLD

OXFORD

TRANSITION TO A GLOBAL SOCIETY

Oneworld Publications Ltd
(Sales and Editorial)
185 Banbury Road, Oxford OX2 7AR, England

Oneworld Publications Ltd
(U.S. Sales Office)
County Route 9, P.O. Box 357
Chatham, NY 12037, U.S.A.

© Landegg Academy, 1993
All rights reserved. Copyright under Berne Convention

A CIP record for this book is available
from the British Library

ISBN 1–85168–039–X

Phototypeset by Intype, London
Printed and bound in Great Britain by
The Guernsey Press Co. Ltd, Guernsey, Channel Islands

CONTENTS

FOREWORD

The First International Dialogue on the Transition to a Global Society is, as its title implies, the first in a series of annual gatherings on a variety of themes relevant to the advance of a global society, in the interests of stimulating high-level interdisciplinary dialogue and interaction, ultimately involving every country in the world. The series is jointly organized by the Landegg Academy, the Vienna Academy, and the University of Maryland, under the auspices of Dr Federico Mayor, Director-General of UNESCO, and Mrs Catherine Lalumière, Secretary General of the Council of Europe.

This particular event took place on 3–9 September 1990 at a time of momentous developments on the international front. The tense situation in the Gulf, later to culminate in a six-week war, was already sending shock-waves around the world. Every day that passed underlined the urgent need to develop the proper machinery for the creation of a truly global society, able and qualified to deal with this and similar conflicts on a world-wide scale.

Other equally important and far-reaching events had occurred less than a year earlier, with the domino-like collapse of almost all the eastern bloc regimes in the space of a few dramatic weeks towards the end of 1989. Less dramatic, but no less significant in the long term, were developments in Western Europe towards the goal of integration, a remarkable step in a region long beset by implacable enmities between individual countries, and one confirmed by moves towards the single European market. The world was also about to experience the overnight disintegration of the Soviet Union and the eclipse of communism, and then the convening of a historic Middle East peace conference in Madrid. These events lay in the future as far as this Dialogue was concerned, but as we go to press they provide further evidence of the inexorable process, with all its negative and positive aspects, that is preparing the way for the transition to a global society.

Although many contributions to the First Dialogue have had to be omitted from this volume owing to space constraints, an interesting cross-section is reproduced within these pages. Clearly all contributions were coloured to a greater or lesser extent by the situation as it stood in September 1990.

Thus the remarks of some contributors can now be seen to have been prophetic given subsequent events, particularly in the Soviet Union and Yugoslavia. The civil war that was about to envelop the latter country represents a striking example of outmoded concepts putting global thinking into reverse, with tragic results.

Perhaps the most salient message to emerge from these papers is that the transition to a global society, whilst undoubtedly possessed of a momentum of its own, requires the most assiduous effort and application from human beings. This means that old attitudes have to be discarded, allowing the true spirit of *glasnost* (openness) and *perestroika* (restructuring) to prevail not only in Eastern Europe but throughout the globe. Above all, the emphasis must be placed on unity in diversity. This, as many contributors make clear, is no mere slogan; the urge to cement peace and harmony can and will resolve conflicts, triumphing over misplaced fears of submerged identity and individuality. Human diversity is a fact, an inescapable reality; the challenge facing humanity lies in establishing unity.

Forging a path to such positive outcomes is what dialogue is all about. For when people of different nationalities, different cultures, different races, different disciplines, come together and discuss the way ahead, the human creative faculty is released, and the achievement of unity and integration becomes genuinely possible. The event that this volume preserves for posterity is, we trust, a small step in that direction.

The editors wish to express their gratitude to Professor James Malarkey for his indefatigable efforts and trenchant perception in recording the proceedings and in summarizing sometimes extremely complex and difficult material. Many others made equally important contributions towards the success of this Dialogue in a variety of different areas of specialization, and we are particularly indebted to the members of the Board of Trustees of the Landegg Foundation: Mr Roger Blaser, Mr Heinz Göltenboth, Dr Marco Kappenberger, Miss Susan Pomeranz, Dr Kazem Samandari and Mr Daniel Schaubacher; also to Mr Walter Webber, Director of Central Administrative Services and the Landegg Conference Centre; Mr René Steiner; Miss Sylvia Fröhlich; Mr Etienne Broder; and the entire staff of the Landegg Academy.

Finally, the most important result of the Dialogue was the formation of a special representative committee and International Advisory Board, consisting of Iraj Ayman, Suheil Bushrui, Ervin Laszlo, Dorothy Nelson, Adamou Njoya and Karan Singh, with its general secretariat in Landegg. This committee, operating under the umbrella of the Association for International Dialogue on the Transition to a Global Society, is empowered to act on behalf of the Association in presenting suggestions and recommendations to governments and international bodies. In particular, its members made a detailed report to the United Nations Conference on Environment and Development (UNCED), also known as the Earth Summit, which took place on 1–12 June 1992 in Rio de Janeiro, Brazil. The committee also contacted all non-governmental organizations taking part in what was the biggest conference of its kind ever launched.

Suheil Bushrui
Iraj Ayman
Ervin Laszlo

INTRODUCTION

Federico Mayor

Our world has been based on two pillars, the pillar of freedom – the essential principle of human action and reflection – and the pillar of equity. Some countries have emphasized the first principle, other countries the second, but most have forgotten about solidarity. I hope that the new Europe can provide the world with a vision of union based on freedom and equity but also taking into account solidarity. Clearly, in a situation where the world has one billion people illiterate, one billion people living below the poverty line, even in misery, it is rhetoric to talk about human dignity and human rights. We must from the very beginning have an understanding of the importance of freedom and equity, but also how important it is that Europe takes into account the least developed countries and those people who live in the shadow of ignorance and conflict.

I am delighted to be asked to participate in this Dialogue. A dialogue means that in one sense we stick to our own views and that, on the other hand, we listen to the views of others. I recall a Chinese proverb that a Chinese member of the Executive Board recommended to me when I took up my functions as Director-General of UNESCO. He said that as nature has given us one mouth and two ears, this means we must listen twice as much as we speak. I also believe that dialogue is the best instrument for probing the future and for coming to new understandings about our role and responsibilities in the coming century. Many will be familiar with the ancient Chinese malediction: 'May you live in interesting times!' Interesting times are indeed dangerous times, but they are also opportunities for us to write surprising pages of history. Someday, when future historians study our 'fin de siècle', I hope very much that they accord us the same spirit of tolerance and sense of perspective applied by present-day historians to the thinkers of the 1690s, 1790s and 1890s. Like our forebears we too are attempting to grapple with the lessons of our own century as we move forward to explore the next one.

What is public? What is private? What is the past? What is the future? These are critical questions, not just of semantic definition but of practical significance in any serious discussion of the role of the public sector in the 'governance of the transition to a global society'. The twentieth century, I think we can say with confidence, provides us with both the apogee of the state in various totalitarian manifestations and with the end of the omnipotent state as an acceptable answer to our problems. It was Erich Fromm who described totalitarianism as 'the escape from freedom'. By this, he meant that the twentieth-century state often reflected mankind's fears of being responsible for its own destiny and, instead, offered to the nation the security of self-confident leaders and ideological rigidity. By exploiting a certain fear of responsibility for the future, totalitarianism promised – in exchange for the surrender of personal freedom – a guaranteed Utopia that would justify the sufferings of the present. As the horrors of this century give way to a more modest and more hopeful sense that we and our contemporaries are jointly responsible for 'the shape of things to come', many of us are coming to recognize that inherited ways of thinking may be obstacles to building the future we want.

The changes in the world that have been accelerating over the past months have reached a new stage even in the context of the crisis in the Gulf that weighs on us all today. For the first time in the history of the United Nations, the Security Council has acted against aggression with the full force of unanimity among its Permanent Members. It has taken almost forty-five years to re-forge the consensus among the victorious allies of World War II. A New United Nations, based on a new set of co-operative relationships, is being born. Let us hope that reason and diplomacy will prevail in this unprecedented effort to keep the peace and uphold the principles of international law.

The challenges that we face in the 1990s and into the next century are at least three-fold. The first challenge is related to environmental protection, with particular emphasis on the ecological impact of present strategies and policies for producing and consuming energy. The second challenge concerns poverty, the growing extent of which not only affects increasing numbers in the developing countries, but also significant minorities throughout the industrialized countries. In addition, the new situation in Eastern Europe has raised the issue of large disparities in wealth within the European region itself. The third challenge concerns reforms of complex systems being undertaken in some countries of the North and the South in the wake of recent political, social or economic developments; reforms and experiments are taking place in Eastern Europe and efforts are being made by certain Third World countries to respond to the debt crisis through a range of social and economic reforms.

Each of these challenges directly involves our local, regional and international capacities to analyse problems correctly, co-ordinate effectively with others, make timely and wise decisions and measure our progress. Although this is far from the exclusive domain of the 'public sector' by any formal definition of the term, it does encompass a more general concept of 'governance'. By governance I mean the integration of our public and private institutions – and, in fact, the integration of our public and private selves – in an effort to create a public projection of our fondest hopes. While there is a Utopian element in this, there is also the practical responsibility to grow and change with the requirements of our times.

The apparent chaos of the world around us is summed up in these three challenges. Each confronts us with a paradigm of instability that can reach a point of irreversibility. The fundamental responsibility of goverance – both public and private – is to act *in time* to avoid the 'points of no return' that would spell environmental catastrophe and a free fall of much of the world's population into absolute poverty or, in some regions, into despair at the chronic failure of political and economic systems to promote economic progress, democracy and respect for the dignity of each human being.

Effective governance requires answers to three sequentially related questions. The first is: 'How much do we really know about these challenges?' The second, of equal importance, is: 'What is the general perception of these challenges among decision-makers and the public at large?' The third is: 'To what extent can we act effectively in the immediate present?' Each of these questions, of course, is an input to practical decision-making.

Over the past decade we have learned much about the interaction between international, national and local economic activities and the accelerating trends that threaten our biosphere. We know that our major ecological problems result from the production of non-recyclable waste. These are products of combustion or industrial processes that cannot be reintegrated into the self-regulating mechanisms of the biosphere. The most important example is the macro-pollution caused by fossil fuel combustion, which has unleashed the phenomenon of global climate change, or the greenhouse effect. Human activity, ranging from the cooking fires of the Third World villages to the automobiles and industries of wealthier countries, have converged to put unprecedented concentrations of carbon dioxide and other gases into the atmosphere. Not only deforestation but also pollution of the oceans have weakened the earth's capacity to reabsorb carbon dioxide, while man-made gases, like chloro-fluorocarbons, are depleting the ozone layer.

We are all aware of the threat of melting ice-caps, rising seas and major changes in rainfall patterns. The question is whether there is time to arrest and reverse these trends before we reach a point of no return. There are many options in energy production; hydro-electric, nuclear, biotechnological and solar sources of energy each must be evaluated in terms of their usefulness in the short term and their environmental impact over the long term. Nuclear power plants could provide a solution if we were able to solve the problems of radioactive wastes, nuclear generator accidents and the potential for the proliferation of nuclear weapons. Photo-voltaics seem to offer a less powerful but more flexible near-term alternative to fossil fuels. But I return to the question in a slightly different form: can we at present say that we know enough about the problem and about the solutions to act without delay? And when we put the problem in this way, what is 'enough'? This is a crucial point, since many vested interests will do their best to keep decision-makers convinced that more knowledge is essential before we take action, and the result will be that necessary measures are needlessly delayed. I would suggest, as a professional biochemist, that the best clinical diagnosis is the one that makes possible a timely treatment. A complete and comprehensive clinical diagnosis is, after all, only possible when the patient has died and we can perform an autopsy.

Poverty, surely a phenomenon related to deforestation and the burning of certain fossil fuels, raises the much broader issue of sustainable development and its potential to create a better life for the majority of people on this planet. It, too, is a rapidly growing problem despite decades of so-called development planning and almost a generation of widespread transfers of technology from the North to the South. Exponential population growth, massive urbanization in the Third World, lack of clean water, uncertain food supplies and, above all, illiteracy and ignorance are all part of this chronic and growing challenge. Technology, in itself, has not provided a convincing answer and it is evident that the cultural aspects of development have not been given adequate attention by the planners. Technology, after all, is not only a scientific application or a machine. It is also a set of social skills and activities that are part of productive community life. Imported technologies often require careful modification and preparation if they are not to have a negative or disruptive effect on their users.

André Leroi-Gourhan has pointed out that the history of technology clearly shows that a social group cannot assimilate a new technology if it has not already mastered the technical developments that went before it. In other words, it is difficult and perhaps dangerous to try to leap to very expensive high technologies without working with cheaper, simpler and more appropriate technologies in the first place. This should not provide an excuse for sharing only 'secondhand' technology with the developing countries. Joint efforts must try to overcome the obstacles that often prevent the developing countries from fully benefiting from advanced technology.

Education – understood as the key to participation in social life – has a crucial role to play in development, but it too must be understood as a medium or, if you will, a technology for the spread of knowledge and skills. It also requires a similarly careful adaptation to its setting and the surrounding culture if it is to make its full contribution to removing certain sources of chronic poverty, for it would be a serious mistake not to see a continual and ascending spiral of human misery as a threat to the well-being and stability of our shared global society. Extremism, violence and desperation take root among those consigned to the level of near subsistence and virtual hopelessness.

The economic and social reforms being attempted in Eastern Europe, as well as in certain Latin American and African countries, are somewhat different forms of challenge. Often a reaction to economies dominated by the public sector, either on a communist model or one of military dictatorship, these reforms seem to be placing an excessive hope in a rapid transition to a free-market model. Undertaken in a context of considerable indebtedness, weak planning institutions and uncertain currencies and markets, the management of such a complex transition is no easy matter, particularly when the historical memory of the 'culture of freedom' is lacking. The free market itself – the so-called 'invisible hand' – is no guarantee of meeting long-term needs or of ensuring the best use of human resources. The question again is whether we possess adequate knowledge to devise sound methods of moving from centrally planned economies to a freer, but nonetheless humane market. A longer-term view based on investing now to prevent future catastrophes is the beginning of a process of placing ethics at the core of our actions. This in my view is most important, for those who have been suffering under the shadow of oppression or extreme poverty will be very disappointed if we offer them only the rules of the free market.

Our perception of these challenges is as important as our understanding of their dynamics. The search for new interdisciplinary and action-oriented approaches requires a social consensus that agrees on the priority to be given to such issues as the environment, sustainable development and efforts to improve living standards among the poorest populations. Pragmatic philosophers and teachers like John Dewey and William James argued earlier in this century that the way in which we state a problem determines how we go about solving it. In other words, the perception of decision-makers and the public at large is a key element in mobilizing resources, research and – most important – resolve, in order to confront the looming threats to human survival.

Here, it would be accurate to say that the perceptions shared at this conference may well be in advance of those in the world around us. This is not a self-congratulatory statement. It is never enough in itself to know more or to see more clearly. It is essential to share knowledge and information effectively, so as to create an informed public and to alert decision-makers to long-term challenges. For, while environmental consciousness is surely on the rise, and such issues as global change are moving upwards as priorities for government action, it is far from certain that sufficient commitment to rapid action will come about 'in time'. Part of the reason for this is the obstacle to a holistic approach posed by the over-specialization of too many disciplines.

Now is the time for natural scientists and social scientists, teachers and artists, communicators and researchers to begin stepping beyond the narrow boundaries of their fields and begin working together and building a dialogue. Only in that way, by transcending what Ervin Laszlo calls the 'introversion' of the specialists, can we share all that we know with the public and the decision-makers.

If scientists have begun to speak out loudly, as they must, on the dangers of a culture, society and economy built on short-term economic interests, others in the fields of education, the arts, social sciences and the humanities must join with them to point out that not only are we confronted with a possibly hostile set of natural trends but that also we must face potentially fatal flaws in ourselves, our values and our way of conducting 'business as usual'. Introversion, while contributing to that private self-knowledge and moral commitment that helps us measure our actions by their long-term results, can cut us off needlessly from the teaching function that all disciplines must perform if the ethical core of democracy is to be developed and strengthened.

Nowhere is this need for mobilizing the best in our secular and religious ethics more dramatic than in confronting the issue of increasing global poverty. Lately, some people have coined the expression 'compassion fatigue' to explain declining public concern with the worsening conditions of so many in the Third World and even in the North. It is argued that the continual presentation of images of mass suffering in the media has had the effect of desensitizing audiences to a problem that is nothing less than a chronic moral outrage. 'Compassion fatigue', let us be quite clear, is an unacceptable form of moral laziness. To combat it we need to devise ways of convincing the public and decision-makers that solutions can be found and that some already exist, ready to be implemented. We must tell the decision-makers and the public at large that we can act, that we have this possibility of providing solutions right now. Certainly the spread of literacy and basic education in the poorest countries is possible, given sufficient international resources and the commitment of the public and private sectors in these countries.

And on this I also insist very much, because in the past two years it is very clear that the awareness among all decision-makers in the industrialized countries that no development is possible with one billion illiterates has led to an extensive consultation of the more important United Nations organizations with the non-governmental organizations. It is essential for us to promote, to mobilize, to facilitate, but it is up to the civil forces to react and to implement these kinds of programmes. And I am glad in this respect to say that recently, at a conference organized by UNESCO with the United Nations Development Programme, UNICEF and the World Bank, not only were declarations of principles and a practical plan of action approved unanimously, but the financing institutions also provided the economic resources to make achievement of the plan possible. We were all glad to hear the President of the World Bank saying that one billion dollars more per year will be available to provide loans for 'Education for All'. We were pleased to hear the administrator of the UNDP saying that it will double and even triple the amount that it is now devoting to education. Yet, if there is not the political will at the national level to shift priorities, to provide more resources for the human needs of all citizens, these efforts will be useless.

In this respect, I must recall that in 1989 the expenditure on armaments of non-industrialized countries, that is developing countries, was $300 billion. Shall it be said that we cannot face the challenge of illiteracy among one billion people? Of course we can, if we provide the guidelines and persuade the decision-makers to shift their priorities. If their priority is to spend $300 billion on armaments, we will then, of course, not have money for matters such as education, health and justice.

The industrialized countries must learn too that sustainable development and global security are chronically endangered by increasing numbers of poor people and their declining hope for progress towards development. The linkages between the issues of energy consumption, global change, poverty, demographics and the need for new approaches must be made clear to as wide an audience as possible. Only in this way can a new sense of global community be forged and 'compassion fatigue' defeated.

The most difficult question is what we must do in the here and now to confront the challenges of our times. The so-called public sector does not and cannot exist in a vacuum, cut off from the ideas, the concerns and the daily activities of private citizens living their so-called 'private lives'. In a crisis – in a period of accelerating instability in human systems and in humanity's relationship to nature – public and private questions converge. Global change will erupt in our lives as it already has in those of drought-stricken farmers in certain regions of the world.

The public sector must therefore be humble and respectful of the expertise and insights of scientists, artists, scholars and teachers who have important experiences to share and important things to say. At the same time, it should actively engage in a process of promoting the freest possible flow of specialized knowledge into decision-making systems. The reflex of bureaucracies, public and private, to look to the well-beaten paths of the past, to 'stay on the rails', wherever they lead, must be changed. The playwright and President of Czechoslovakia, Vaclav Havel, said in an interview with the *Unesco Courier* that: 'Alive and mysterious, reality transcends all imaginable theories, plans and concepts. To order and organize it calls for humility and respect for the richness, the diversity, all the colourful variety of life.'

By breaking down its own walls of bureaucracy and introversion, the public sector can lead the process of seeking holistic visions of the world around us. The fact that almost forty-five years ago, the victorious allies of World War II created an international organization dedicated to things of the mind and the spirit should be seen as an early attempt by the public sector to transcend its limits. UNESCO's constitutional commitment to create the defences of peace in the human mind by working for co-operation among public and private institutions reflects a vision that may only be within our grasp today. Yet we must remember that the immediate post-war generation had hopes for transcending the public and the private. Linking the world of ideas and the world of decisions was seen as an essential foundation for building a peaceful and dynamic world community.

That dream could not be achieved in a world divided into hostile ideological and military camps. UNESCO could not live up to its full potential in a global situation characterized by a culture of war. I remain convinced that we stand at the threshold of a new culture of peace. With the improvement in the capacity of the United Nations to fulfil its peace-keeping role, a parallel development may be a renewed capacity for international intellectual co-operation to imbue public matters with private, moral imperatives and creativity.

With humility and respect for the complexity and the richness of the life that goes on around us, meetings such as this one can weave a tapestry of public and private resolve to know more about the challenges facing us, help people to perceive them better and move rapidly towards concerted action.

The need to 'think globally and act locally' also has a temporal meaning. Our locality is the present. Our globality is the flow of time and evolution from past to present to future. As a species, this means very special responsibilities for educating young people about the environment around them and about the plight of so many of their brothers and sisters throughout the planet. Holistic approaches among the next generation may be the best guarantee of linking science, technology, social science and art into new forms of communication, new ways of learning and innovative approaches to action. UNESCO stands for dialogue – between adults and children, scientists and poets, scholars and schoolteachers – on a global scale. As such, it stands ready to move the dialogue from this setting outwards to networks and classrooms throughout the world. For it is words and ideas and questions that will take us forward to the future and meet the challenges of this twentieth-century 'fin de siècle'.

Federico Mayor, the recipient of numerous awards and honours, has held the post of Director-General of UNESCO since November 1987. He is a former Rector of the University of Granada and Minister for Education and Science in Spain, who has served in the European Parliament and published scientific articles and reports in international reviews.

PART 1

THE
EVOLUTIONARY CONTEXT
OF THE
TRANSITION

SCIENCE AND OUR
UNDERSTANDING OF THE WORLD

Ilya Prigogine

I

Science plays an enormous role in today's world. But we are living, to use a well-known expression coined by C. P. Snow, in a society of 'two cultures', the arts and the sciences. Communication between the people of these two cultures is often difficult. What is the reason for this dichotomy? I believe it lies in the way the conception of time is incorporated into each of these cultures.

Time is our fundamental existential dimension. It has fascinated artists and philosophers as well as scientists. The incorporation of time into the conceptual scheme of Galilean physics marks the origin of modern science. However, in this scheme time appears in a quite restricted way, as no distinction is made between past and future. In all phenomena we deal with, be they in macroscopic physics, chemistry, biology, or the human sciences, future and past play different roles. There is an arrow of time, but how can this arrow of time emerge from 'non-time'? Is time as we perceive it an illusion? The paradox of time is the subject of this talk.

Can we contrast being with becoming, as we contrast truth with illusion? The discussion in Plato's Sophist bears testimony to his own hesitations: 'We communicate, you say, with becoming by means of the body through sensations, whereas we communicate with true being by means of the soul through reasoning; and truth, you say, is always in the same unchanging state, while becoming behaves sometimes in one way, sometimes in another.' This has also been the position of classical physics. Its task was to discover the unchanging, beyond constantly changing appearances. Plato's Sophist emphasizes the paradoxical character of this position: it would exclude life and thought from the realm of being. Plato concludes that we need both being and becoming.

Over the whole history of western thought the same problem has been faced again and again. Lucretius introduced the 'clinamen', which perturbs the fall of atoms in the void, in order to allow for novelty. This appeal to the clinamen has often been criticized as the introduction of a foreign element into the world of atoms. Two thousand years later, we read in an Einstein paper, dealing with the spontaneous emission of light by excited atoms, a similar statement: 'The time and direction of the elementary processes are determined by chance.' This is a most unexpected parallelism if we remember that Lucretius and Einstein are separated by what was probably the greatest revolution in our relations with nature, the birth of modern science.

Newtonian science introduced the concept of 'changeless change'. Physical change was expressed in terms of laws that ignored the difference between past and future. Isabelle Stengers and I wrote in *Order Out of Chaos*:

> 'like Aristotle's gods, the objects of classical physics are concerned only with themselves. They can learn nothing from the outside. At any instant, each point in the system knows all it will ever need to know, that is the distribution of masses in space and their velocities. Each state contains the whole truth concerning all possible states, and each can be used to predict the others, whatever their respective positions on the time axis. In this sense, this description leads to a tautology, since both present and past are contained in the present.'[1]

But Plato's riddle was not solved. Even Einstein, one of the strongest supporters of classical determinism, felt compelled to reintroduce unpredictable events into his description of the spontaneous emission of light. Since then, the duality between 'laws' and 'events' remains at the centre of physics as it has been at the centre of philosophy since Plato.

It is interesting to analyse the concept of a 'law of nature', so fundamental in western science. We have become so used to it that it seems almost a truism, something that goes without saying, but it is absent in other world-views. According to Aristotle, living beings are not subject to laws. Their activity results from their own autonomous internal causes. Each living being is striving to achieve its own specific truth. In China, the dominant view was that of a spontaneous cosmic harmony, a kind of equilibrium linking nature, society and the heavens. The idea that the world may be submitted to laws emerged gradually in western thought. Its origins can partly be associated with the Stoics, through their insistence on fate. But an essential role has been played by the Christian God conceived of as an omnipotent legislator.

An important moment here was the sixth-century dispute between the Christian John Philoponus and the neo-Platonist Simplicius, whose commentaries and quotations are one of our main sources for Greek philosophy. Let us listen to Simplicius' reaction to Philoponus' ideas:

> How could anybody with a normal mind possibly conceive of such a strange God, who first does not act at all, then in a moment becomes the creator of the elements alone, and then again ceases from acting and hands over to nature the generation of the elements one out of another and the generation of all the rest out of the elements?

Indeed this was a strange thought for a Greek, but it was a natural consequence of Philiponus' conception of God as creating the world *ex nihilo* and as apprehending temporal things in a timeless way.

For God, everything is given. Novelty, choice or spontaneous actions are relative to our human point of view. This conception has dominated classical science. As Leibniz wrote: 'In the least of substances, eyes as piercing as those of God could read the whole course of the things in the universe, *quae sint, quae fuerint, quae mox futura trahantur.*' The discovery of nature's unchanging laws was thus bringing human knowledge closer to the divine, atemporal point of view.

This programme has been immensely successful. The explanation of every natural phenomenon in terms of deterministic laws seemed to be at hand. These deterministic laws introduced a number of different types of interactions. Classical physics knew gravitational as well as electromagnetic forces. Modern physics added strong nuclear as well as weak interactions. Physicists are still working on their unification. The hope has been the discovery of a single law from which all others could be derived. This hope was at the origin of Einstein's work on unified field theory. It still forms the main theme of Stephen Hawking's recent book, *A Brief History of Time.*[2]

And yet, since the nineteenth century, the emergence of sciences based on different paradigms has opened new perpectives. Both thermodynamics and Darwinian biology are evolutionary sciences. Thermodynamics is closely associated with the industrial age, when a deep anxiety was created by the rapid transformation of our relations with nature. It seemed that the universe was doomed to evolve towards 'thermal death', the levelling of all differences. Biology, since Darwin, is also the expression of an evolutionary paradigm, but Darwinism emphasized the appearance of novelty: new species, new modes of adaptation, new ecological niches.

With the emergence of these evolutionary paradigms, the time paradox has entered the realm of science. On one side, in classical Newtonian science there is no arrow of time, on the other, the concept of irreversibility is central to thermodynamics as well as to biology.

The first scientist to confront the time paradox was the Austrian physicist Ludwig Boltzmann, who attempted to link the 'arrow of time' introduced by thermodynamics with classical dynamics. Boltzmann failed, and this failure led him to conclude that the difference between past and future was an illusion due only to the inherent limitations of our knowledge. Let us quote Karl Popper's protest, echoing Plato's criticism againt those who wish to contrast being and becoming:

> I think that Boltzmann's idea is staggering in its boldness and its beauty. But I also think it is quite untenable, at least for a realist. It brands unidirectional change as an illusion. This makes the catastrophe of Hiroshima an illusion. Thus it makes our world an illusion, and with it all our attempts to find out more about our world. It is therefore self-defeating (like every idealism).[3]

The origins of physics were marked by an irreducible contingency. Nature seemed to answer the questions asked by the great founders of modern science such as Galileo or Newton, and so confirmed the legitimacy of their approach. However, we can now better appreciate how much these great achievements were based on the specific nature of our environment. Take, for instance, the motion of the earth around the sun. The history of physics was decisively influenced by the fact that the interactions between the earth, the moon and the other planets can be neglected in a first approximation when we study the motion of the earth around the sun. If not, the earth's orbit could not have been described as a two-body system (earth–sun), and the heavens would not have offered us the spectacle of simple periodic motions. Perhaps a probabilistic approach would have been proposed to describe the complexity of planetary motion. Perhaps also the idea of unstable dynamic systems would have surfaced much earlier. We do not owe to cultural convictions alone the grand theoretical visions of classical physics; we also owe them to the fact that, in our complex environment, simple situations could be singled out, capture our attention and inspire the creation of adequate languages to describe them.

Today, physics is capable of overcoming the specific circumstances of its birth. We can admire the simplicity of planetary motion but we now better understand its particular, almost singular, character. It is this transformation of our point of view that I intend to describe here. I would like to share with our readers the feeling that we live at a privileged moment. Physics is now at a threshold: it opens up a world of new questions, and at the same time leads us to a better understanding of its history.

II

The last decades of our century have seen a resurgence of interest in the time paradox. Most of the questions Leibniz and Newton discussed are still with us, particularly the question of novelty. How can we account for novelty without denying it, without reducing it to a mere repetition of the same? Jacques Monod deserves credit for fully emphasizing the conflict between a concept of laws of nature that ignore evolution and the production of novelty. How then can an event such as the origin of life be understood? For Monod the appearance of life was a statistical miracle: our number has come up in the cosmic game of chance.[4] But the scope of the problem is even wider. The very existence of a structured universe presents a challenge to the second law of thermodynamics: Boltzmann concluded that as a result of the second law of thermodynamics, the only normal state of the universe corresponds to 'heat death'. All other states could only be understood as temporary fluctuations.

'Will we be able some day to overcome the second law?' This is a question that people, from generation to generation, from civilization to civilization, keep asking the giant computer in Isaac Asimov's story *The Last Question*.[5] The computer has no answer: 'The data are insufficient.' Billions of years pass by, stars and galaxies die, but the computer, now directly connected to space–time, continues to collect data. At last no information can be gathered any longer, nothing 'exists' any more, but the computer continues to calculate, to discover correlations. And finally it reaches the answer. There is no longer anyone there to learn, but the computer now knows how to overcome the second law. And there was light . . .

Like the appearance of life for Jacques Monod, the birth of the universe is thus conceived by Asimov as an anti-entropic, 'anti-natural' event. But Asimov's victory of knowledge over the laws of nature or Monod's cosmic game of chance are ideas of the past. It is no longer necessary to think that the events to which we owe our existence are foreign to the 'laws of nature'. These laws are no longer opposed to the idea of a true evolution that includes novelty. For them to be able to do so, we have to show that they fulfil three minimal requirements.

The first is irreversibility, the breaking of symmetry between past and future. But that is not enough. Consider a pendulum whose motion gradually comes to an end, or the moon, whose period of rotation on its axis has progressively decreased. Another example would be a chemical reaction, whose rate vanishes at equilibrium. Such situations do not correspond to true evolutionary processes. A second requirement is needed: we have to introduce the idea of an event. By its very definition an event cannot be deduced from a deterministic law: it implies, in one way or another, that what happened did not necessarily have to happen. This implies the need for a probabilistic approach. However, even probabilities are still not sufficient. A history is worth telling only if some of the events it describes generate 'meaning'. A succession of throws of dice has no story to tell unless some throws have consequences in the future, for instance if the dice are part of a game of chance and if the throw decides between winning and losing.

Everyone knows the story about the weak nail whose breaking entailed the loss of a horseshoe whose loss stopped a horseman whose absence caused defeat in a battle that led to the fall of an empire . . . This type of question fascinates every lover of history and is a major theme of science fiction's 'journeys in time': what would have happened if . . . ? Such a question always presupposes a change in scale. A seemingly insignificant event could have changed the course of history. Thus, the third requirement we have to introduce is that certain events be capable of transforming the course of evolution. To put it another way, evolution must be characterized by mechanisms able to make some events the starting point of a new development, of some new global coherence.

Darwin's theory of evolution illustrates well all three requirements we have stated. Irreversibility is obvious: it exists at all levels, from the birth and death of individuals to the appearance of new species and of new ecological niches that lead in turn to new possibilities for biological evolution. The striking event Darwin's theory had to explain was the appearance of a new species. But this event itself is described as the result of complex processes. In order for it to occur we need a class of micro-events: a population is made up of individuals which, even if they belong to the same species, are never identical. The birth of each individual therefore constitutes a micro-event, a small modification of the population. The appearance of a new species signifies that, among all these micro-events, some acquire a special meaning: certain individuals are, for one reason or another, characterized by a higher rate of reproduction, and their multiplication gradually transforms the average characteristics of the population. Natural selection thus corresponds to a mechanism by which small differences can be amplified and eventually produce the true novelty, the appearance of a new species.

The Darwinian approach only supplies us with a model. But every evolutionary model must likewise involve irreversibility, events, and the possibility for certain events to become the point of departure for a new coherence. History is not reducible to underlying regularities nor to a simple collection of events. Every historian knows that the study of the exceptional role of single individuals implies the analysis of the social and historical mechanisms that made this role possible but also that without the existence of these individuals – a particular event – these same mechanisms could have generated a very different story.

Thermodynamics as formulated in the nineteenth century was centred around the idea of equilibrium. It did not describe evolution in the same sense as did the Darwinian model. It is true that the preparation of a far-from-equilibrium system could be considered an event, but traditional thermodynamics only described the way this event is 'forgotten' while the system evolves towards its equilibrium state.

However, over the past twenty years thermodynamics has undergone considerable changes. The second law of thermodynamics is no longer limited to the description of the levelling of differences that marks the approach to equilibrium. It is worth describing in some detail this conceptual transformation, which brings the problem of becoming into the heart of physics.

We will not dwell here on the discovery of the so-called 'dissipative structures' as described in Order Out of Chaos.[1] Let us only recall that it was predicted theoretically and verified experimentally that a class of physicochemical systems presents, when we increase the distance from equilibrium, transitions to states characterized by space–time coherence. The discovery of such 'structures', which exist only as long as the system dissipates energy and therefore produces entropy, was quite unexpected, and the name we have given to them, 'dissipative structures', emphasizes the close association they imply between aspects of equilibrium that thermodynamics opposed: the dissipation due to the entropy producing activity and the structure this dissipation was thought to destroy.

The two fields of science where dissipative structures are studied most are hydrodynamics and chemical kinetics. Let us first consider an example in hydrodynamics, the 'Bénard instability'. A thin layer of liquid is subjected to a difference of temperature between its lower surface, which is kept heated, and its upper surface, at room temperature. For a small temperature difference, that is near equilibrium, the heat is transferred only by conduction, that is through collisions among the molecules. Above a well-defined threshold of the temperature difference, there appears in addition a transfer of heat by convection. This means that the molecules then participate in collective motions that correspond to vortices dividing the layer of liquid into regular 'cells'.

The appearance of these Bénard vortices corresponds to a breaking of spatial symmetry. Before the onset of the collective motions, each layer of the fluid was in the same state. That is no longer the case when the Bénard instability takes over: at one point in space the molecules rise, at another they fall. How is this possible? How can molecules suddenly evade incoherent thermal motion? This was the great surprise provoked by the discovery of dissipative structures: no new force is introduced. It is because of the sole thermal constraint we apply to the liquid layer that the same molecules interacting through random collisions are able to switch to coherent collective behaviour.

As has been shown, the appearance of this coherence is due to long-range correlations that exist between molecules in non-equilibrium conditions. Matter at equilibrium is blind. Far from equilibrium it begins to 'see'.

Let us next consider an example taken from chemical kinetics.[4] In this case, the constraint imposed on the system refers to its chemical composition: it determines a deviation from the equilibrium composition. Chemical reactions proceed through collisions between molecules.

A much-studied example corresponds to the appearance of chemical clocks far from equilibrium. As long as chemical constraints are maintained, the reaction proceeds in a time-periodic fashion, in spite of the thermal motion which tends to randomize the temporal evolution of the system. Periodic transformations again involve billions and billions of molecules. Therefore, exactly as in the Bénard convective vortices regime, the system then forms a 'whole' in which each part is 'sensitive' to all the others.

Chemical oscillations break time symmetry. They proceed in a sequence oriented in time (contrary to a frictionless pendulum). In addition, many space-symmetry-breaking structures have been observed over recent years. We now observe the appearance of 'dissipative crystals' (Turing structures) whose lattice distances are macroscopic in contrast with equilibrium crystals whose lattice distances are of the order of angströms (10^{-8}cm). The lattice distance in non-equilibrium crystals is the result of complicated interplay of reaction rates and diffusion coefficients. The lattice sites are the points where one of the chemical reactants has its maximum concentration.

It is difficult to imagine a better example of order generated by irreversible processes than dissipative 'crystals'. Far from equilibrium, irreversible processes may thus be a source of coherence, the very condition for the formation of 'dissipative structures'. This forces us to reconsider what we call a 'system'. Whereas the behaviour at equilibrium or near equilibrium is, at least after a sufficiently long period of time, completely determined by boundary conditions, the situation drastically changes far from equilibrium.

Many different dissipative structures are compatible with the same boundary conditions. This is a consequence of the non-linear character of far-from-equilibrium situations. Therefore, the 'choice' of the state that will be realized is no longer determined by the boundary conditions. This is one of the reasons why we have to ascribe to such systems a certain 'autonomy' or 'self-organization'.

What would have happened if. . . ? This question obviously concerns historians. It now also concerns physicists studying a system that they can no longer describe as controllable. Such a question, which makes the difference between a narrative science and a purely deductive one, does not refer to insufficient knowledge but to the intrinsic behaviour of a far-from-equilibrium system at *bifurcation points*. Those are the critical threshold points where the behaviour of this system becomes unstable and can evolve towards several branches corresponding to different stable modes. No 'increased knowledge' will ever make us able to predict which mode it will adopt.

The simplest bifurcation point corresponds to a situation where a state becomes unstable while two other possible stable states emerge symmetrically. This case illustrates well the irreducible probabilistic character of bifurcations, a breakdown of deterministic behaviour that refers to the macroscopic level. There exists one chance in two of finding the system beyond the bifurcation point in one or the other of its two possible modes of activity. The outcome of the bifurcation is as random as a throw of the dice.

The theory of bifurcations is now in full bloom, and many names are associated with it, especially that of René Thom, whose theory of catastrophes led to one of the first classifications of the possible types of bifurcation. One of the most surprising results of this new development is the great diversity of situations that arise far from equilibrium. When we drive a system away from equilibrium, it may pass through multiple zones of instability. In each of them its behaviour changes in a qualitative way. In particular it can reach a 'chaotic' state, a state whose behaviour best symbolizes the renewal of the concepts of order and disorder that far-from-equilibrium physics imposes on us, since it is both coherent, implying long-range correlations, and unpredictable.

III

We have been speaking of macroscopic physics. But we cannot describe the world around us without taking into account the constructive role of time. The problem that remains is to make the transition to the microscopic world without losing this essential aspect. We have already mentioned Boltzmann's struggle to incorporate the second law of thermodynamics into the framework of classical physics. We have seen that he was forced to conclude that the irreversibility inherent in thermodynamics was incompatible with the reversible laws of dynamics.

Physics, for most of the twentieth century, seemed to prove him right, as both relativity and quantum mechanics agreed with classical dynamics in denying time. But a dramatic change has now taken place. As a testimony of this change let us quote the solemn declaration made in 1986 by Sir James Lighthill, at the time president of the International Union of Theoretical and Applied Mechanics:

> Here I have to pause, and to speak once again on behalf of the broad global fraternity of practitioners of mechanics. We are all deeply conscious today that the enthusiasm of our forebears for the marvellous achievements of Newtonian mechanics led them to make generalizations in this area of predictability which, indeed, we may have generally tended to believe before 1960, but which we now recognize were false. We collectively wish to apologize for having misled the general educated public by spreading ideas about the determinism of systems satisfying Newton's laws of motion, that, after 1960, were to be proved incorrect.[6]

This is a quite unusual confession. Historians of science are used to 'revolutions' in which one theory is defeated, while another comes to dominate. But it is quite rare to see experts recognize that for three centuries they were mistaken regarding the scope and the significance of their own field! Indeed, the renewal of the oldest of our sciences during the past few decades is a unique event in the history of science. Determinism, which for a long time appeared to be the very symbol of scientific intelligibility, is today reduced to a property valid only in limiting situations. Furthermore, probabilities, which Boltzmann felt compelled to turn into the expression of our ignorance, acquire now an objective significance.

The important point is the discovery of chaotic systems even in simple situations. The fact that regular behaviour can become 'chaotic' is not a novelty: a classical example is the transition between laminar and turbulent flow. But a fluid is a complex system made up of an immense population of interacting particles – a system we clearly cannot hope to describe in terms of individual trajectories. Similarly, the model Boltzmann adopted to interpret the second law of thermodynamics supposes a large number of particles. In such situations, physicists had to proceed by approximations, and they thus could feel justified making irreversibility the result of the approximations. On the contrary, as we see it now, the notions of chaotic behaviour and of temporal horizon apply already to simple dynamic systems that we can rigorously describe.

The temporal horizon of a chaotic system creates a basic difference between the 'now', the individual system whose behaviour we can predict using our present and past knowledge, and the 'hereafter', an evolution that we can no longer describe in terms of individual behaviour but only in terms of the behaviour common to all systems characterized by the same chaotic attractor. This difference is an objective one: it does not refer to any contingent practical limitation and puts no limit on the sophistication of our measurements.

We know now that all dynamical systems, be they classical or quantum, are not alike. This insight goes back to a basic theorem established by the great French mathematician Henri Poincaré almost one century ago. In a somewhat schematic way, we may say that Poincaré's question was: can we 'eliminate' interactions in dynamic systems? Systems for which this is possible were called 'integrable' by Poincaré. Integrable systems are therefore by definition isomorphic to systems of free particles. But are all dynamical systems integrable? If Poincaré's answer had been positive, no bridge would have been possible between a world described in dynamic terms and our world with its coherence, its chemical and biological processes. Fortunately, the fundamental theorem formulated by Poincaré in 1889 shows that in general dynamical systems are 'not integrable'. Interactions cannot in general be eliminated.

Poincaré's theorem shows that all dynamic systems are not alike. All dynamic systems studied in elementary textbooks are integrable. This includes two-body motions such as the earth–sun problem. However, already three-body systems are not integrable. Poincaré has shown why dynamic systems are not integrable and interactions cannot be eliminated. The reason is the occurrence of resonances. The idea of resonances is a familiar idea; as children, we already know how to amplify the motion of a swing using resonance. Poincaré proved that resonances lead to divergences when we try to eliminate interactions: this is the 'small denominators' problem, which was already known to the founders of classical mechanics such as Lagrange and Laplace. They knew that in our planetary system there are resonances that lead to secular effects. Poincaré considered the occurrence of divergences as the result of resonances as the basic unsolved problem of dynamics. First this problem had attracted interest only in a restricted circle of specialists. It was considered as a technical problem that would ultimately be solved by applying sufficient mathematical ingenuity. However, the situation changed drastically with the formulation of the so-called KAM theory (KAM referring to Kolmogorov, Arnold and Moser) around 1950. In short, KAM theory has shown that resonances lead to two types of trajectories: trajectories that behave 'normally', in the way we are used to studying planetary two-body motion, and trajectories that behave randomly.

With the increase of randomness we come to 'chaos'. An enormous amount of work has been devoted over the past few years to describing the paths that lead from normal trajectories to chaos. We want to emphasize that KAM theory has not, however, solved the problem of Poincaré's divergences. It has led to a classification of trajectories. We need to go further. It is a quite remarkable fact, only recently noticed, that there are also non-integrable systems in Poincaré's sense in quantum mechanics and that Poincaré's divergences appear there as well.

For decades Poincaré's divergences have been considered as an obstacle, as expressing the difficulty of applying methods that had been proved highly successful for integrable systems. For us, Poincaré's divergences were an opportunity to build a bridge between two continents, to achieve a formulation of dynamics valid for unstable dynamical systems. We have shown that we can indeed eliminate Poincaré's divergences but that this elimination leads to a formulation of dynamics that incorporates, from the start, irreversibility and probability – two basic elements needed to describe the macroscopic world around us. Therefore the elimination of Poincaré's divergences solves the time paradox. But it does much more, as it leads to a formulation of dynamics that incorporates irreversibility and chaos.

In *Science and the Modern World*, Alfred North Whitehead wrote that modern science described the physical world as 'a dull affair, soundless, scentless, colourless, merely the hurrying of matter, endless, meaningless'.[7] This 'dull affair', however, has led to the most demanding quest for knowledge. I have been describing part of this quest.

In his recent book, *A Brief History of Time*, Stephen Hawking concluded that once the 'complete theory' of the universe was discovered, the only remaining question would be 'why it is that we and the universe exist. If we find the answer to that, it would be the ultimate triumph of human reason – for then we would know the mind of God'.[2] Then indeed we would share His non-temporal vision of the universe, and we would understand the eternal necessity beyond the appearances of becoming.

Hawking's view reflects the traditional conception of what may be the ultimate goal of physics. In the past, physicists have often stated that all great problems would soon be solved and theoretical physics would come to an end. This end is identified with the discovery of some 'theory of everything', a nearly magic super-law out of which we could deduce all forms of physical reality from elementary particles and photons to black holes. The theory of everything would reduce the universe to some identity, to some basic geometrical, timeless description.

Emile Meyerson has seen in the attempt to reduce nature to an identity the main driving force of western science.[8] He described how again and again nature has disappointed the hope of those who believed in a possible reduction to an identity. For Meyerson the second law of thermodynamics, and therefore the arrow of time, was the symbol of the rebellion of nature against reductionist rationality. Furthermore, he emphasized that intelligibility, in the context of the quest for identity, annihilates what it was meant to grasp. What remains of our relation with the world if this world is reduced to some geometrical truth?

At, the end of his life, Einstein was offered a collection of essays[9] that contained among others a contribution by the great mathematician Godel. Godel had taken quite seriously Einstein's conviction that time as irreversibility was only an illusion. He presented to Einstein a cosmological model in which travel back to one's own past were possible. He even made an estimate of the quantity of fuel needed. Einstein was not enthusiastic. In his answer he wrote that he could not agree because he could not believe that a person could 'telegraph back in his own past'. He even added that this impossibility should lead physicists to reconsider the problem of irreversibility. For Einstein, whatever the temptation of the eternal, to accept the possibility of travel backwards in time was to deny the reality of the world. He could not go along with this radical endorsement of his own views.

We find a similar reaction in a beautiful text of the great writer Jorge Luis Borges. In *A New Refutation of Time*, he describes the doctrines that make time an illusion and concludes:

and yet, and yet . . . Denying temporal succession, denying the self, denying the astronomical universe, are apparent desperations and secret consolations [. . .] Time is the substance I am made of. Time is a river which sweeps me along, but I am the river; it is the tiger which destroys me, but I am the tiger; it is a fire which consumes me, but I am the fire. The world, unfortunately, is real; I, unfortunately, am Borges. Time and reality are irreducibly linked. To deny time may be a consolation or may appear as a triumph of human reason. It is always a denial of reality.[10]

As mentioned, Stephen Hawking believes that we are close to the moment when we shall read the mind of God, close to the end of science. However, the statement that we are now close to the 'end of science' may also take another quite different meaning. The 1989 Nobel Conference at the Gustavus Adolphus College (St Peter, Minnesota) was entitled 'The End of Science', but the meaning of this expression was far from optimistic. The organizers wrote: 'As we study the world today, there is an increasing feeling that we have come to the end of science, that science, as an universal, objective endeavour, is over.' They went on: 'If science does not speak of extra-historical, universal laws, but is instead social, temporal and local, then there is no way of speaking of something real beyond science, that science merely reflects.'

This statement echoes Einstein's belief; if science is not a 'mere reflection' of reality as it exists beyond us, if science is part of human history, objectivity is lost. Science would be only one subjective enterprise among others. Our thesis is quite the opposite. The great laws of physics are not 'mere reflections' of reality, but they are also not mere 'social' or 'historical' constructions. The classical ideal of objectivity, and the denial of time it implies, has no extra-historical status. It emerged from western culture in the seventeenth century. But this ideal does not correspond to arbitrary judgements that we would be free to maintain or to give up at will.

The idea of objective physical reality as exemplified by dynamic description was the result of the first successful attempt to incorporate time into a mathematical scheme. More than two centuries, between Galileo and Boltzmann, were needed to understand the price to be paid for this achievement: the contradiction between the basic laws of physics, on the one side, and all processes characterized by a broken time symmetry on the other.

Today, physics recognizes the arrow of time as an essential property of reality. The intrusion of time in physics does not herald any loss of objectivity or of intelligibility. On the contrary, it opens the way to new forms of intelligibility.

This incorporation of probability and irreversibility in dynamics can certainly not, however, be deduced from some extra-historical necessity. The arrow of time would not have penetrated into the basic level of physics without the invention of new questions, without the search for an opportunity to solve the time paradox. The notion of opportunity refers to science as a human, historical dialogue with nature, a dialogue in which symbolic thought plays an essential role.

Human creativity is essential in the history of science. Strangely enough, scientific creativity is often underestimated. Everyone knows that if Shakespeare, Beethoven or Van Gogh had died in infancy, nobody would ever have achieved what they did. Is this true for scientists? Would not somebody have discovered the classical laws of motion if there had been no Newton? Did the formulation of the second law of thermodynamics depend on Clausius? There is some truth in this contrast. Science is a collective enterprise. The solution to a scientific problem must, in order to be acceptable, satisfy exacting criteria and demands. These constraints, however, do not eliminate creativity.

Some scientific achievements are indeed great surprises. There is no reason to believe that without Einstein we would have general relativity, without Planck, quantum theory. The science of the twentieth century could have been the pursuit of the excellent research programme as formulated at the end of the nineteenth century. We believe with Paul Valéry that 'dans la phase la plus vivante de la recherche intellectuelle, il n'y a pas de différence, autre que nominale, entre les manoeuvres intérieures d'un artiste ou poète, et celles d'un savant'.[11]

This unpredictability of the history of science has part of its origin in nature. This was denied by some philosophers, and first of all by Kant. For Kant, nature as interrogated by the scientist cannot surprise him. It is like a witness answering the questions the judge is asking, and only these questions. In order to make sure that the judge would never meet a surprise, Kant stated that phenomena as we observe them are products of the categories of our own understanding. Nature as a witness is thus a priori submitted to the very laws in terms of which it is interrogated.

The history of science has not followed the course Kant predicted. It has not been an endless confirmation of the Newtonian scheme. Nature has indeed the power to surprise us. Who would have thought that matter consisted mainly of unstable particles? Who would have foreseen the possibility of an evolutionary universe? Who would have imagined the marvellous structure of the DNA molecule? Science is not a unilateral questioning of nature but a dialogue with nature.

The notion of 'laws of nature' made us inheritors of a conception of nature which, as we have already emphasized in *Order Out of Chaos*, was deemed very naive in a civilized country like eighteenth-century China. Was Nature 'obliged' to follow these laws, somewhat as a good citizen obeys the laws of his country?

This is indeed the ideal expressed in the notion of 'laws of nature', an ideal that expels us from the world we claim to understand. For Einstein, any deviation from this ideal meant giving up the ambition to 'understand' the world, the very project of science. This corresponds obviously to a very peculiar interpretation of what 'understanding' means. The master who believes he understands his slaves because they obey his orders and follow the rules he imposes would be blind. Where living beings are concerned,

be they horses, dogs or cats, we do not identify understanding with obedi-
ence to rules. We would refuse to recognize as a real cat one whose
behaviour we could always predict. Even in physics, Nabokov's conviction
remains true: 'What can be controlled is never completely real; what is real
can never be completely controlled.'[12]

What is completely random, however, also lacks reality. We have to find
a narrow passage somewhere between two conceptions that both lead to
alienation. One is the conception of a world ruled by laws that leave no
place for novelty and creation. The other is the conception symbolized by
a dice-playing God, the conception of an absurd world, where there is
nothing to be understood. It is a symbol for despair, which may lead us to
the stoic attitude of Jacques Monod, discovering a universe from whence
we emerged by chance, a meaningless universe, deaf to our music, or to
our anger, as for Shakespeare's Macbeth.

What is emerging is an 'in between' description, which involves both
laws and events, regularities and randomness.

The great French poet Paul Valéry has written that he wished his work
to be 'a preface to a theory of time'. Time, for him, was construction. This,
I believe, gives some hope for humanity at this difficult moment of transition to the twenty-first century.

References

I would like to thank Isabelle Stengers and Dean Driebe for their help in
preparing the manuscript.
1. Prigogine, I. and I. Stengers, *Order Out of Chaos*. New York: Bantam, 1984
2. Hawking, S., *A Brief History of Time*. New York: Bantam, 1989
3. Popper, K., *Unended Quest*. La Salle, Ill: Open Court Publishing, 1976
4. Monod, J., *Chance and Necessity*, transl. by A. Wainhouse. New York: Vintage
    Books, 1971
5. Asimov, I., *Robot Dreams*. New York: Berkley Books, 1986
6. Lighthill, Sir J., *The Recently Recognized Failure of Predictability in Newtonian
    Dynamics*. Proc. Roy. Soc. Lon, A 407, b.35–50, 1986
7. Whitehead, A. N., *Science and the Modern World*. New York: The Free Press,
    1964
8. Meyerson, E., *Identity and Reality*. London: Allen and Urwin, 1930
9. Einstein, A., *Philosophic-Scientist*. P. H. Schlipp, ed. New York: Tudor, 1949
10. Borges, J. L., *A New Refutation of Time*. London: Penguin Books, 1970
11. Valéry, P., *Cahiers*, Pléiade. Paris: Gallimard, 1973
12. Hayles, N. K., *The Cosmic Web*. Ithaka: Cornell University Press, 1984

Ilya Prigogine is a Professor Emeritus at the Free University of Brussels.
Professor Prigogine received the Nobel Prize for Chemistry in 1977 for his

research into 'dissipative structures'. He is a member of a wide variety of leading academies and scientific professional organizations and has received numerous honorary doctorates and awards.

BUILDING A GLOBAL SOCIETY: PROGRESS AND PROCEDURES

Robert Artigiani

I

Lord Bolingbroke defined history as 'philosophy teaching by example'. There is, however, no consensus on what historical lessons philosophy teaches,[1] for everyone aspiring to teach lessons uses different perspectives to interpret examples. The lesson I would like this 'Dialogue On the Transition To A Global Society' to consider depends on a perspective borrowed from contemporary science. Interdisciplinary borrowings must be treated tentatively, so my aim is mostly to stimulate discussion. But I believe that history teaches us to analyse the processes facilitating social evolution instead of trying 'to identify as clear a vision as possible of a feasible and desirable future'. Enticing as 'a feasible and desirable future' is, human societies represent 'incomprehensible information' defying clear identification. The focus of our considerations, therefore, should be on describing rules for how societies evolve.

The history of the US Constitution provides an example of this lesson. Denounced by Mercy Warren as 'a Republican form of government, founded on the principles of monarchy' upon which 'a democratic branch with the *features* of aristocracy' had been stuck, the document has survived to become the oldest written constitution in use. Since its ratification, tens of millions of immigrants have swept through its structure, the thirteen seaboard states that crafted it have swollen to a continental colossus, and a sparsely populated Arcadian garden has become an urbanized industrial society.

The history of this transition is as uninspiring as any. The original states threatened repeatedly to withdraw from the Union, and a bloody civil war was fought to preserve it. Class and racial conflicts have often been more intense than those of other western countries, while the nature of political debate has usually displayed a lamentable propensity for ideological rigidity. In other words, despite natural advantages, as people Americans have behaved no better than most and worse than some. America's successful evolution, therefore, probably depends largely on the rules for change written into the Constitution of 1787.

It would be presumptuous to claim the US Constitution should be the basis for organizing a global society. Nevertheless, interpreted from the perspective of dissipative structures theory,[2] American social evolution does appear to follow patterns of self-organization found in other parts of nature. Without wishing to be too simplistic, I think this conclusion makes the convergence of the natural and human sciences possible, since nature's capacity for organizing increased complexity implies that humans are not prisoners of their biological inheritance and that genuinely progressive change is possible.

The recent discovery in chaos theory of 'obstacles' to predicting the future of complex structures, even when the rules determining their behaviour are known,[3] is equally important in facilitating social evolution. Obstacles to prediction deny the quasi-scientific basis of commitments to idealized futures[4] and may reduce the propensity of 'true believers' and 'terrible simplifiers' to impose Utopian blueprints on humanity by force.[5] But if we cannot know the future, we are inescapably part of a present allowing no moral alternative to action. It is reasonable, in such circumstances, to follow Bolingbroke's advice and seek, in the historical example of a nation that organized itself without obliterating the identities of its disparate units, useful lessons about the transition to a global society.[6]

II

Viewed as evolutionary structures, societies create a new level of reality, breaking the symmetry of biological evolution in the same way that biology breaks symmetry in chemical evolution. Moreover, social structures must be treated as whole systems. They 'emerge' at discontinuities when random 'events' produce 'laws' that organize behaviour in qualitatively new ways that can redefine their human components. Since, however, organizational laws are undetermined by the histories of their systems, we seem trapped between an ethical obligation to solve problems and the realization that we cannot entirely succeed.

The sciences of self-organization, however, suggest there is room to dance between the horns of this dilemma. This possibility follows from the fact that social systems, like biological organisms, are preserved far from equilibrium as identifiable entities by their internal constraints. Internal constraints, such as the grammars that make languages adaptive, restrict lower-level possibilities. Constraining lower-level possibilities, in turn, makes freedom real by making choices meaningful.[7] Without grammatical rules, there would be no communication. But as long as only the mechanics of communication are restricted, we are free to choose what we say. Grammars constrain *how* we speak without dictating *what* we say.

Languages, however, are also whole systems. They are self-referential, each symbolic representation referencing others in a seemingly endless chain, which, Niels Bohr was fond of remarking, leaves us 'lost in a sea of words'. There is no perceptible link between verbal representations and external 'reality', which is just another word.[8] But admitting that external reality cannot be directly accessed from within a language system does not deny there is a reality beyond language. In fact, it is logical to suppose that natural selection operates on languages and societies as it does on biological organisms. Different societies will have attributes that advantage or disadvantage them selectively. One of those attributes will be the languages with which they co-evolve.[9] A people will flourish or suffer, survive or perish, at least in part because of the language they speak. Thus, people speak languages and languages speak people.

Presumably, the internal constraints organizing a social structure are as relevant to its selective opportunities as they are to a language. Therefore, modelling strategies for social transitions on language-like processes may be reasonable. Concentrating on the mechanics or procedures – the 'grammars' – for regulating *how* societies do things, overall system behaviour would be freed to explore a maximum of environmental possibilities. Then new information can be generated by the society reading its environment and effectively adapting to it by choosing *what* to do from the bottom up.

Procedures are means to achieve ends, but by reversing Machiavelli's priorities I am not claiming that means are value-free. On the contrary, procedures, like tools or technologies, put purposes into concrete form. Procedures are culturally embedded; they are always selected with certain goals in mind. Their very existence implies the value of a goal, as linguistic grammars imply the value of communication. Moreover, as B. L. Whorf pointed out,[10] linguistic structures affect the ability to express ideas and shape the consciousness of speakers. Similarly, the procedures through which the behaviour of a social whole is orchestrated will load the dice in favour of some propensities and against other possibilities.

In other words, societies have identities. They are not at equilibrium and they act purposefully. Their purposes partly derive from goals and values that appear, at least, to be independent of the particular methods constituting specific societal procedures. But in the non-linear world of social systems, it is impossible to isolate ends and means. Procedures are values incarnate, and values are shaped by procedures. A procedure is chosen because it can accomplish a goal, and successful societies pursue goals within methodological reach. When procedures embody standards for evaluating and redefining goals as environmental realities alter, peaceful evolution towards more complex social structures may be enhanced. That is, orchestrating behaviour around fair procedures can trigger adaptive responses while preserving societal functions during transitions to new behaviours.

By focusing our strategy on the syntactic rather than the semantic level of society, goals can remain extremely general: for example, to 'form a more perfect Union, establish Justice, insure domestic tranquility, provide for the common defense, and secure the Blessings of Liberty to ourselves and our Posterity'. General goals adjust speedily to altered environmental conditions. It may even be possible, by partially dissociating procedures from specific goals, to modify the ends so that new means can be used. Then procedures can evolve along with society, like languages, as ends and means feed back on each other. The example of the US Constitution supports this philosophical lesson.

III

The US Constitution was written as the newly independent republic, foundering amidst debts and sometimes violent internal conflict, reached what Hamilton called 'almost the last stage of national humiliation'. No better than most national leaders, the handful of men closeted in Philadelphia aimed to write a constitution that would give the nation a formal identity. In fact, as Charles Pinckney pointed out to them, the delegates in Philadelphia began their discussion in a fantasy world where America was constantly confounded with contemporary Europe and with ancient Greece or Rome. But as the delegates met, they quickly discovered there was no shared sense of what the national identity should be. Each of them had different ideas about the nature of the collective whole and different predictions about its future.

Dividing the delegates were profound differences between those who aspired to a hierarchical society reflected in an aristocracy, and those whose egalitarian values aspired to democracy. Such aspirations had practical consequences. Some led to a centralized nation, others to a fragmented one; some to slavery, others liberation; some left the big states dominant, others preserved the autonomy of the small; some implied a commercial society, others an agricultural one. Overriding all concerns were differences between those most anxious to avoid anarchy and those most fearful of despotism.

Finding from the start that its delegates disagreed, the Convention was in danger of failing before it began. But Washington, Franklin, Madison and others artfully reconstructed the agenda. It was clear to them that the delegates were legislating for the future. But Washington knew their work could not be 'perfect' in anyone's eyes. 'I do not think we are more inspired, have more wisdom, or possess more virtue than those who will come after us', he wrote. Franklin wisely recognized that 'we must not expect . . . a new government may be formed, as a game of chess may be played, by a skilful hand, without a fault. The players of our game are so many, their ideas so different, their prejudices so strong and so various, and their particular interests, independent of the general, seeming so opposite, that . . . chance has its share in many of the determinations, so that the play is more like *tric-trac* with a box of dice.'

Realizing the limits of their situation, Madison actually rejoiced in the fact that Utopian visions were unrealizable, that, in the words of the intrepid traveller Arthur Young, a constitution was not 'a pudding to be made by a recipe'. 'Would it be wonderful if, under the pressure of all these difficulties', Madison wrote, 'the Convention should have been forced into some deviations from that artificial structure and regular symmetry which an abstract view of the subject might lead an ingenious theorist to bestow on a constitution planned in his closet or in his imagination?'

Once the Founders realized they were unable to identify a clear vision of what the new nation *ought* to be, they settled for formulating the mechanisms by which the United States, over time and through experience, would *define itself*. They abandoned dreams of producing a Utopia and, in the words of the antifederalist William Manning, 'spent 4 months in making . . . an inexplicit thing . . . a Fiddle, with but few strings'. Aware that 'Reason may mislead us', the Founders, said John Dickinson, were immune to the allures of Platonism and made 'Experience . . . our only guide'.

Abandoning the endeavour to create a national *society*, the Founders instead described a national *government*. In effect, they de-coupled the behavioural expression of the social whole from the legal machinery of political life.[11] Guided by mechanical images, enshrined, for instance, in the separation of powers, the Founders intended to make a Newtonian 'machine that would go of itself'.[12] They succeeded beyond their wildest dreams, for the effect of their efforts solved Von Neumann's problem by creating a machine able to build a machine more complex than itself. In the language-like organism that emerged from a series of compromises, the Founders actually laid the basis for an evolutionary social system.[13]

Realizing they could not produce a model as complex as existing reality, the Framers did not confuse their map with its territory. Their Constitution, like a grammar, establishes the rules for making rules, the laws of the game rather than its outcome. For example, the Constitution is purposely vague about why officials should be impeached, but very precise about how to impeach them. Similarly, legislative procedures are spelled out with almost algorithmic clarity, although neither the kinds of laws that should be passed nor the judiciary's role in determining their 'constitutionality' is specified. In the most famous example, the Constitution requires 'due process', but – if decades of lawyerly debate are any indication – never says what 'due process' is. 'No legislative act . . . contrary to the Constitution, can be valid', as Hamilton said. But the spectrum from precisely descriptive, authoritative language to language more open to interpretation is continuous. This strategy frees future generations to choose the kind of nation they want, as long as the procedures agreed upon at Philadelphia are followed.

Moreover, the Bill of Rights keeps America 'error friendly',[14] at least to a degree. That is unexpected for, from the point of view of a social system, individualized behaviours violating established norms are mistakes, not creative acts. Most societies suppress deviations, for they are conservative systems homoeostatically attempting to preserve existing structure. But errors, like newly minted metaphors, are critical to adaptation. They allow environmental dynamics to be continuously explored. As the environment changes, some mutated representatives of the system, at least, may be fit to survive in new conditions. African-Americans were only counted as three-fifths human and women were denied any public life in 1787, but later Americans were not tied to past prejudices. Abolitionists could advance the thirteenth amendment, which liberated slaves, and Suffragists campaign for the nineteenth, which granted women the vote.

Lincoln, debating with Douglas over slavery, showed how treating the nation like a language permits expression to evolve over time. Lincoln knew slavery was constitutional, of course. But he claimed the very act of constituting a society revealed a desire to improve it. Slavery was an evil that existed when the Constitution was written, and tolerating it was one price paid for establishing a society. But Lincoln believed the society was created, in part, to correct evils in the future. Thus, he could argue that when the Declaration of Independence proclaimed 'All men are created equal', the ideal was irrelevant to 'effect[ing] our separation from Great Britain'. Rather, it was stating a 'standard maxim for a free society, which should be familiar to all, and revered by all, constantly looked to, constantly labored for, and even though never perfectly attained, constantly approximated, and thereby constantly spreading and deepening its influence, and augmenting the happiness and value of life to all people of all colors everywhere'.

As rights, the values of freedom and equality formally stand outside the Constitution, drive the system it organizes, and make possible the normative restructuring of the behaviours defining American society. To be sure, fired by emotional commitments, people and groups will contest who shares rights and to what extent, and, by formalizing the rules of constantly shifting power-centres, the Constitution endorses factional competition. Using, according to Madison's prescription, 'ambition . . . to counteract ambition', the nation's behavioural structure approximates to a heterarchy, a system whose hierarchical relationships are not rigidly fixed but alter over time as the relative power of its component parts alters to meet varying crises. Flexibility permits new opportunities to be exploited, as demonstrated by the vast reserves of energy and talent released by moving towards racial and sexual equality. Thus, following Constitutional procedures allows the fulfilment of ethical aspirations to track the evolution of complexity, for the farther from equilibrium a society is, the more dependent upon the initiative of fully developed autonomous individuals it becomes.

IV

As the 'cement of the Union', as Madison called it, the Constitution supplied internal constraints that preserved a destabilized structure far from equilibrium. Recording information created by debating, ratifying, and implementing the Constitution, the American nation emerged as a self-organized societal whole. No external power, divine or natural, wrote the Constitution; a handful of Americans sat down and sketched the relationships that would structure the nation to which they aspired to belong. Then the populace edited the sketch in the process of implementing it. The Founders were, after all, trying 'to protect the minority of the opulent against the majority', as Madison conceded. They may also have been, as Jefferson argued, so 'much impressed by the insurrection in Massachusetts' that they set 'up a kite to keep the henyard in order'. But public outcries led to amending the initial document with a Bill of Rights, showing how non-linear causal processes work, unpredictably, to redefine a possibility as popular support amplifies it. Cascades of popular feedback from the stimulus of the proposed new Constitution led immediately to changes in it, changes whose implementation entrenched the system in its human environment. The Constitution no more created the nation as its linear causal effect than the nation – which did not even exist – created the Constitution. Both emerged together, forming and being formed by one another. Based on the 'consent of the governed', the constitutional system is, like a language, self-referential. It is the 'consent of the governed' that justifies the acts of 'we the people', and the 'consent of the governed' is achieved because the Constitution obliges even a majority of 'we the people' to obey fair rules of play.

By finding solutions that eluded the Founders, recursive applications of the Constitution give Americans a national identity, making the Constitution the kind of template familiar to the sciences of self-organization. It ceases to be the tool for searching out an identity and becomes its basis. Successfully balancing local needs and interests, collective use of Constitutional procedures encourages their internalization by succeeding generations. As Tocqueville noted,[15] for instance, every time Americans join together for any purpose, they write a constitution for their group. Correlating actions around the procedures originated in Philadelphia, the Constitution, in Jefferson's term, becomes 'the text of civil instruction'. 'A constitution', according to John Adams, 'introduces knowledge among the people and inspires them with a conscious dignity becoming to freemen; a general emulation takes place which causes good humor, sociability, good manners, and good morals to be general.' The people, as Montesquieu had expected, mould the instrument of government that afterwards moulds the people.

The identity derived from the US Constitution provides transitional societies with a built-in capacity for evolution. The Constitution is 'in the first instance a set of ways of living and doing' that 'generates attitudes not only of general and specific approval . . . but also . . . built-up predispositions in the participants, to deal with situations those participants have previously never met or thought of, *along the lines* of the ways they know . . .'.[16] Thus, when altered environmental conditions provide a new context in which to evaluate social behaviour, the self-referential relationship between a people and fair procedures for societal self-correction periodically folds the society back on the Constitution. Then the standards of fairness incarnated in the rules of procedure serve as the established criteria for judgement, and the subtle relationship between co-evolving system levels becomes apparent.

Instrumental procedures are transparent during stable periods. At symmetry-breaks, however, the method for achieving implicit goals becomes visible as fundamental law. The Constitution then forces Americans to evaluate collective action reflexively by explicitly identifying the medium of societal expression with the content of its behavioural message. The society is effectively 'deconstructed'[17] and can be reorganized to model an expanded environmental niche. Against a new environmental background, previously excluded people and unperceived problems are illuminated. Their protests, voicing demands for Constitutional protections through Constitutional mechanisms, force American society to evolve qualitatively by pursuing the rights and liberties said by Lincoln to have originally inspired the act of constituting. Stability is regained by altering social relationships explicitly to embody rights and liberties the earlier structure had not recorded. Nor is there an obvious limit on evolutionary progress, since the behavioural message expressed by the societal whole is ultimately modelled on the grammar constraining its relationships, and grammatical constraints leave expression open-ended.

V

The example of the US Constitution teaches that clear visions of the human future are unnecessary and undesirable. The clearer the vision put forward, as the spokesmen for the Virginia Plan quickly learned, the more opposition it is likely to generate. But if our goal really is the establishment of a just society on a global scale, and if we internalize the perspectives of dissipative structures and chaos theories, then we realize our choices must be made amidst ambiguity and doubt. Random events and obstacles to prediction put us all behind the 'veil of ignorance' postulated by John Rawls as the heuristic device for defining justice.[18] None of us knows where we will stand in the future, although we know our present positions cannot determine the outcome.

This situation is actually liberating,[19] for in moving towards a new global system, we need not know what Truth transcends time nor articulate it independently of space. On the contrary, the lesson of philosophy taught by the example of Philadelphia is that what we need to do is 'constitute' the public arena[20] in which future generations solve their own problems. By forming the mechanisms of government, the Philadelphia Convention performed that basic function. Raising, in Washington's words, 'a standard to which the wise and honest can repair', it established the rules by which subjective selves relate to one another.

No clear vision of the future, shaped as it inevitably must be by cultural biases, could 'raise the standard' to which all who are 'wise and honest can repair'. But honest people support rules of fair play, and wise ones see the utility of previously agreed procedures in an evolving world. In environments as dynamic as those selecting for or against contemporary societies, they must constantly 'learn' or perish. Societies learn by modelling their environments, and they model environments by locating people hierarchically. When the environment is dynamic, and the model constantly changing, it makes little sense to worry about how a society is formed; that is, about where in it individuals or classes are momentarily located. For in dynamic environments societies 'think'[21] by 'making-up new people'[22] as the relationships defining them shift. People will, at one time, be members of a dominant network and, at other times, be shifted to subordinate positions. The critical point, therefore, becomes the 'justice' with which people are brought into and released from various behaviour patterns.[23] What is critical is establishing procedures for fairly deciding such issues, for setting the boundaries of the public space.

In a public space protected by procedural rules, 'men', in Madison's terms, do not have to be 'angels'. They do not even have to be good. Madison's great insight was simply that each of us is bound to be controlled by private interests and that we will inevitably join with others similarly inclined to advance our views. His, and Hamilton's, is a Hobbesian analysis.[24] But the individual sinners lamented by the Founders can be transformed into the virtuous community they ardently desired by the process of interacting publicly. The wonderful result of their factional conflicts, Madison argued, is that when procedural rules constrain factional competition, the ensuing compromise reflects the collective good. Now, of course, to individuals, public compromises rarely look virtuous. Rather, they look like sell-outs. But that may merely be the consequence of looking at the behaviour of the whole from the reductive perspective of one of its parts. Our private perspectives, uncluttered by external inputs, usually seem clear, for we are each in the position of Franklin's friend at the French court for whom '*Il n'y a que moi qui a toujours raison*'. If we attempt to impose our private perspectives upon the world, however, community is lost.

But perhaps Madison was right and we need neither win every battle completely nor identify a clear view of society. If we do in fact establish and respect rules of fair play, the basic procedures by which we interact in all our subjectivity, then our confidence in one another builds, along with a shared identity, because each of us is protected in our differences as our needs are reconciled. The law then stands above ourselves, and the blending of our subjective interests in respecting law gives it an objective status.[20] Needs may never be completely satisfied. But they do not have to be, so long, Madison said, as 'the private interests of every individual may be a sentinel over public rights'. When individual interests guard the rules of fair play, the rules permit us to renew the struggle in the future. As long as the procedures for interacting are themselves above factional revision, we can preserve faith in the system itself, in the constituted public space, despite specific solutions to particular problems. Regardless of the form society takes at any moment, faith in how society functions can sustain community.

Using commonly agreed procedures creates the public experience upon which community, like language, rests. Procedural rules are an interface between individuals making the exchange of information possible. When information is exchanged, the meaning of relationships is established. Individuals, or factions, encode their identities in action, which are decoded by the responses of others within the society. Meaning resides in the 'difference'[25] between people, which makes individuals or groups 'valuable' in terms of one another. Thus, concentrating on the mechanisms of communication does not ignore the emotive or affective realm of human interaction. For, as in the domain of language, once the rules of communication exist, people can be as emotional or poetic as they wish. But shifting the focus of our considerations to the grammatical rules organizing societies, the freedom of future generations to write, in the language of changing social forms, whatever societal poem they wish is preserved.

The life of a nation is expressed in its actions. When America's Founders established procedures constituting a public space, they provided the means by which successive generations would decide for themselves what America 'means'. This decision exemplifies the 'larval thinking' advocated by Prigogine and Stengers.[26] As the larva 'is not autonomous and organized *vice* a world to which it must adapt' but 'constitutes itself in a very process of constituting its relation to the world', so in obeying the rules of procedure Americans make the choices expressing the nation's identity in forms varying with circumstance. The habits cultivated in the public space shape the behaviour defining the nation. It is for this reason that the 'fundamental law of the land' adapts by mapping a variety of territories.

VI

Twentieth-century societies are in greater peril than America was in 1797. Their tendency, as in most 'times of troubles', has been to search for perfect, permanent, and rigid responses. The Stalinist or Nazi systems show that millions may be killed in pursuit of these 'final solutions', but results are short-lived and counter-productive. The more modest work of Philadelphia may be closer to the language-like processes of nature, for by concentrating on strong procedures rather than ultimate goals, a functioning democracy was built that has lasted over two hundred years. From the perspective of history as self-organization, philosophy teaches that we are creatures of the structures we make. Structures produced in accordance with preconceived blueprints too often twist their makers into victims. Structures created by following rules of fair play enhance the humanity of those who dwell within them, for the 'wise and honest', the actions of millions of East Europeans demonstrate, 'will repair' to systems whose evolution permits them to define themselves.

References

1. Barber, S. A., *On What The Constitution Means*. Baltimore: Johns Hopkins University, 1984; Eidelberg, P., *The Philosophy of the American Constitution*. New York: Free Press, 1968
2. Prigogine, I., *From Being to Becoming*. San Francisco: Freeman, 1980
3. Devaney, R. L. and L. Keen (eds.), *Chaos and Fractals*. Providence: American Mathematical Society, 1989
4. Roque, A., 'Safe-Fail Justice' in Proceedings of the International Society for the Systems Sciences, unpublished manuscript, 1990
5. Popper, K. R., *The Open Society And Its Enemies*. New York: Harper, 1962
6. Van Doren, M., *The Great Rehearsal*. New York: Penguin, 1948
7. Pattee, H. H., 'Hierarchy Theory: The Challenge of Complex Systems', in H. H. Pattee (ed.) *Hierarchy Theory*. New York: Braziller, 1973
8. Rorty, R., *Contingency, Irony And Solidarity*. Cambridge: Cambridge University Press, 1989
9. Hillis, W. D. 'Intelligence As An Emergent Behavior; or the Songs of Eden,' *Daedalus*, (no. 1) 117: 175–190, 1988
10. Whorf, B. L., *Language, Thought And Reality*. New York: Wiley, 1956
11. Berthoff, R. and J. M. Murrin, 'Feudalism, Communalism, and the Yeoman Freeholder: The American Revolution Considered As A Social Accident', in S. G. Kurtz and J. H. Hutson (eds.) *Essays On the American Revolution*. Chapel Hill: UNC Press, 1973
12. Kammen, M., *A Machine That Would Go Of Itself*. New York: Knopf, 1987
13. Wilson, W., *The New Freedom*. Garden City: Doubleday, Page & Co., 1913
14. Weizacker, E. and C. F. von, 'How To Live With Errors: On The Evolutionary Power of Errors', *World Futures*, 23: 225–35, 1987
15. Tocqueville, A. de, *Democracy in America*. New York: Vintage 1954
16. Llewellyn, K., 'The Constitution As An Institution', *Columbia Law Review*, vol. 34, no. 1, 1931
17. Schlag, P., 'Le Hors de Texte – C'est Moi,' unpublished manuscript, 1990. Winter, S. L., 'Indeterminacy and Incommensurability in Constitutional Law', *California Law Review*.
18. Rawls, J., *A Theory Of Justice*. Oxford: Oxford University Press, 1971
19. Allen, P. M. and M. Lesser, 'Evolution: Learning About the Importance of Ignorance', unpublished manuscript, 1990
20. Arendt, H., *On Revolution*. New York: Viking, 1963
21. Douglas, M., *How Institutions Think*. Cambridge: Cambridge University Press, 1986
22. Hacking, I., *Restructuring Individualism*. Stanford: Stanford University Press, 1985
23. Wohlmuth, P. and L. Goldberg, 'Justice And The Crisis of Human Membership', Proceedings of the ISSS Conference, unpublished manuscript, 1990

24. Hofstadter, R., *The American Political Tradition*. New York: Vintage, 1973
25. Atlan, H., 'Uncommon Finalities', in W. I. Thompson (ed.) *Gaia: A Way of Knowing*. Great Barrington, Mass: Lindisfarne Press, 1987
26. Prigogine, I. and I. Stengers, 'The New Alliance', *Scientia* 112: 319–312; 643–53, 1977

Robert Artigiani is Professor of the History of Science at the United States Naval Academy. He is a founding member of the General Evolution Research Group and the Washington Evolutionary Systems Society.

THREEFOLD HARMONY AND SOCIETAL TRANSFORMATION

Pentti Malaska

I

In his address to the conference, Ervin Laszlo pointed out the importance of the interplay between processes of diversification and processes of integration in society and world order. Describing these concepts in the terms of evolutionary dynamics, we may speak of *autocatalytic, replicative processes* within different 'orders' in society, on the one hand, and *cross-catalytic, interactive processes* between those 'orders' on the other.

A new kind of process may emerge from the interplay of these autocatalytic and cross-catalytic processes, which may be called a global process. However, the interplay may or may not occur in a harmonious way; the various processes may not reach a matching resonance. If they do not, the form and patterns generated are short in duration and limited in scope. An evolutionary hypothesis can be put forward that it is precisely the harmony (or resonance) of the interplay that makes for better or worse sustainability and globality.

II

The threefold model
A society is here assumed to consist of three diversified human 'orders' or production faculties, each one autonomous and autocatalytic in its existence and function. These three constitutional orders, or 'sectors', are the economic order, the socio-political order and the spiritual order.

The orders are autocatalytic and self-replicative, meaning that economic production has a tendency to generate more economic production; socio-political activity enhances socio-political activity; and the spiritual function produces more spiritual function. Each order feeds itself and replicates through its own specific type of activity.

Economic order

Economic activity absorbs natural resources from the environment and produces material welfare, especially for those who are engaged in economic activities. It invests a share of its production to produce more economic activity; this constitutes the autocatalytic part of the economic function. Unfortunately, by the necessity of natural laws, the economic order also produces harmful side effects, including pollution and destruction of the natural environment, which are in proportion to the magnitude of welfare generated.

We may ask whether some improved, more nature-oriented technology would be possible; whether our material existence could be in better harmony with nature. Ideally, the exchanges between the economic sector and the external environment will try to maximize beneficial products and minimize harmful ones. I will leave this question unelaborated here, and refer to my essay, 'Nature-Oriented Technology.'[1]

Each of the three constituent parts also interacts with the others, in a cross-catalytic manner. Some part of the produce of the economic order must be contributed to the other two orders, as necessary inputs for their production and function. The economic order likewise receives contributions from the other two orders. This general pattern applies for the relations between all three sectors. The exchange of inputs constitutes the cross-catalytic process within society.

Socio-political order

The socio-political function of society clearly forms a domain of its own. Its purpose is fundamentally different from the economic production of material wares, yet its manner of operation is analogous to the economic sector.

The socio-political order consists of all a society's coherent, purposeful activity directed towards the production of socio-political 'wares'. These include systems of justice, equality and security, systems for the provision of health care, laws for the protection of life and human rights, and other social codes governing conduct. Socio-political activity is thus a productive function.

The socio-political order produces these codes of behaviour also to meet demands in its own sector, in an autocatalytic process. From the widespread problem of burgeoning bureaucracy, we know that the socio-political order has a very strong autocatalytic, self-replicative nature. It may be said also to produce waste, that is, too much bureaucracy and obstacles to human freedom.

Spiritual order

The spiritual or cultural functions – the sciences, the arts, religion, education, and so on – produce ideas, values, inventions and expressions of human attitudes. These spiritual functions give meaning to our lives, teaching us to be a humane; or they pollute our reality by pathological attitudes and destructive values. Spiritual and cultural 'wares' enhance further spiritual activity, as well as affecting the economic and socio-political sectors.

The cross-catalytic interaction of the spiritual order with the other orders is the most important source of renewal for human existence. If it is too weak, human existence becomes purely materialistic or bureaucratic. However, the danger also exists that life can become too spiritual, merely a world of fantasies.

III

Harmonious interplay

The functional and productive entities here called the economic, socio-political and spiritual orders work and should be capable of working more or less autonomously; they are by their very nature independent of each other to a large degree. Indeed, this is how they must operate if their full potentials are to blossom. When each of them is performing optimally, they obey different principles. Optimal spiritual functioning is achieved by individual freedom of creation and expression. Optimal economic functioning is reached through disciplined solidarity (and sustainability); and optimal socio-political functioning demands observance of the principle of equal rights for all humans.[2]

Freedom in the spiritual order keeps the door open for the widest diversity of human expression. Solidarity and sustainability in the economic order help to generate material diversity and effectiveness on all levels (regional, national, and local). Equality of rights in the social order promotes a just and stable polity. Not coincidentally, these principles correspond with the ideals of the French Revolution: *liberté, egalité, fraternité.*

A society as a whole will be harmonious, or inharmonious, according to the quality of relations and interactions between its three parts. When there is a harmonious relation and interaction between the diversified orders, it brings a beneficial resonance. Ilya Prigogine highlighted the significance or resonance effects at this conference. The three sectors of society – like tuning forks that transfer energy most effectively to one another when they vibrate at the same frequency – will exchange the maximum amount of energy when they are in a harmonious interplay.

Integration of orders means exchange of their special 'wares' in interaction between them. If the integration is not harmonious, no resonance is achieved; the result will be dissonance, and the whole will sooner or later suffer, and perhaps collapse. It is the harmony, the resonance that creates the capability for evolution. A resonance effect implies replication and amplification of each sector's energy within the societal whole. In resonance the total evolutionary force is at its maximum compared with total energy flow.

Harmony also signifies the absence of dominance of any one of the three orders over the others. The dominating order asserts its own priorities over the other orders, forcing them to obey its own principle of optimization and efficiency. It prescribes tasks to the other orders and imposes its own criteria of effectiveness.

Disharmonies

Dominance is an imbalance that ruins the autonomy and optimal functioning of the subordinated orders. Certain concrete examples may serve to elaborate the point.

1   The western industrialized countries are often regarded as the epitome of materialism, where only economic health and material welfare matters. This characteristic is becoming more pronounced and widespread nowadays, as capitalism flourishes.

The economy is the dominant order in these western societies. The resultant lack of harmony produces alienation from cultural life, lack of societal and spiritual values, and – on a global scale – a widening gap between those who have and those who have not. Because of this imbalance, currently we may speak of transition to a global economy through western dominance, but not to a global society. Within themselves, the western industrialized societies are, however, closer to resonance than any other societies.

2   In contrast to the 'western advance', we are now experiencing the collapse of societies based on dominance of the socio-political order over the economic and spiritual orders. The ex-socialist countries of Eastern Europe lacked harmony and caused human suffering in this way. They were dominated by socio-political orders determined by small elite groups. Transition to a true global society will remain impossible as long as such unbalanced societies remain. In China, one quarter of humanity still lives under a system dominated by the socio-political order.

3   Certain countries in the Muslim world, such as Iran, serve to demon-

strate societal dissonance of the third kind, because of the marked dominance of the spiritual order. Such societies may also become unstable, waiting only for a strong trigger force to cause a breakdown.

4 Certain African societies illustrate what happens when none of the sectors makes an adequate contribution to the societal whole. For example, in most sub-Saharan African nations, development policies have historically favoured urban interests at the expense of rural masses; this can be regarded as a severe shortfall in the socio-political sector. In the cultural sector, the sharply limited capacities of African science and technology contribute to material poverty and social instability, as do inappropriate values inherited from imported education systems and advertising campaigns. In all three sectors, there is often a strong fragmentation of functions due to rivalry among tribal and clan interests.

IV

Societal transformation

Now I turn to the second evolutionary frame, which depicts the internal dynamics of a progressive society as it grows and changes its basic character over time. By societal transformation I mean a self-transformation of the society that builds on new characteristics emerging within the harmonious threefold whole. Achieving a high degree of harmony, resonance and an absence of dominance, the society will attain the requisite effectiveness in resource use and become capable of transmutation.

The general framework for this exploration of societal transformation is the theory of complex, self-organizing systems, far from equilibrium. Important contributions in this field have been made by such contemporary thinkers as Ilya Prigogine, G. Nicholis, Peter Allen and Ervin Laszlo.[3] They have found that all systems tend to follow a similar pattern as they evolve. Laszlo recently summarized this discovery as follows:

> In the most general terms, systems evolve when they reach a sufficient level of complexity, have flexible feedbacks between their components, are exposed to a sufficiently rich and constant source of energy, and when their normal functioning is disturbed. The factor of disturbance – termed 'fluctuation' or 'perturbation' in the thermodynamic theory – is the evolutionary trigger.[4]

When the right sort of disturbance occurs at the moment ripe for change, it has a 'nucleating' effect. It forms a nucleus around which evolutionary change expands, and eventually transforms the entire system.

The guiding hypothesis of my dynamic model is that, in the evolution of human societies, nucleation happens only as new needs arise and begin to be satisfied. The new needs, as they arise, are the key fluctuations, the essential nuclei for change. They may be regarded as intentional forces pulling the transformation process, whereas the prevailing economic, social, and spiritual orders, which generate the new needs, are the causal forces conditioning and pushing the process.

Thus, one may observe world-wide historical patterns of transformation from a society of basic needs (characterized by the dominance of the agrarian mode of production). The typical contemporary classification of societies as agrarian (or pre-industrial), industrial, and post-industrial does not refer to the most basic element in transformation dynamics – need satisfaction. This is why I use a need-based classification instead.

The transformation process has, again, an autocatalytic part and a cross-catalytic part. Taking first the transaction from the society of basic needs (agrarian society), we observe an autocatalytic process in which the wealth and prosperity produced by agriculture are used to improve agricultural productivity.

Initially the most challenging problem of the basic needs of society lies in increasing production through expansion of its resource base (land area, number of cattle, and the like). Providing food, clothing and shelter, as much as possible and as quickly as possible, to as many people as possible, is the main theme: a policy of extensive growth. For much of mankind, the policy of extensive growth of food production is fundamental to the improvement of quality of life even today. However, for the industrialized and industrializing world it has not sufficed for decades.

As time passes, agriculture becomes linked cross-catalytically to non-agricultural activities. Productivity of agriculture starts to increase many times over once it acquires better tools for cultivating and harvesting, manufactured fertilizers, machines for dairies and mills, and so on; that is, when agriculture starts to assimilate inputs from outside itself. Mechanization and the use of chemicals allow the intensification of agricultural production. It is no longer necessary to add to the acreage of cultivated land or the number of cattle, because each acre and animal yields more than previously.

Sooner or later, embryonic industry advances and begins to develop its own autonomous, commercial and economic life, separate from agriculture. It starts to grow, to replicate autocatalytically. This early industry, created in the first place to serve agriculture's needs for tangible goods, becomes the nucleus or 'germ' of regenerative growth. The tangible needs it fosters acquire a momentum of their own.

Regenerative growth is the period of dramatic societal evolution, and it cannot be taken for granted. Only if the proper conditions prevail, including Laszlo's four factors of evolution, will agricultural society experience this type of growth. The germ of embryonic industry played a twin role in the societal transformation of the basic needs society.[5] On the one hand, it was an increasingly important external aid to agriculture that made basic need satisfaction increasingly unproblematic; on the other hand, industry is increasingly able to absorb the surplus of agriculture (production, labour, capital) and to take its place as the dominating force for further change. The industrial way of organizing, producing, and valuing penetrates everything in society, and agriculture will begin more and more to resemble a branch of industry.

The further process of transformation from a society of tangible needs (industrial society) to a society of intangible needs (post-industrial society) follows a logic analogous to that of the transformation from the society of basic needs to one of tangible needs. The production and use of information, with its associated services, is the nucleus of the transition. Information is not the product of industry. Rather, it comes from outside the industrial mode of production, and triggers intensive growth in industrial production.

During the stage of intensive growth, industry produces more from less; it conserves capital, labour, raw materials, energy, space and the environment while improving quality and service. This stage of intensive growth, which we are now witnessing in the most industrialized countries, may well be called an 'information society' phase, or a 'super-industrial phase'. It is not a question of a post-industrial society as yet, but only an intensification of the industrial society. The objective remains the same: satisfaction of tangible needs with manufactured wares.

The new welfare accumulated during the extensive and intensive growth periods of the industrial mode of production can be channelled again into the fulfilment of new needs. Information and information technology are as important for the satisfaction of some types of intangible needs as shovels and power engines are for the satisfaction of certain tangible needs. The emerging orientation to intangible needs influences the mode of production, which becomes increasingly orientated to services, human interactions, and information. As industry and agriculture become increasingly efficient and unproblematic, they are penetrated by the service function; they become a branch of services, so to speak.

However, there is a great gap of 'unfilled intangible needs' in the advanced societies that cannot be filled by information technology. In the society of intangible needs, new problems and new potentials will challenge people in ways that are scarcely imaginable now.[6] Questions of employment and increased international interdependence loom large, as does the frightening prospect of totalitarian social control.[7] The new science of complexity will be necessary for understanding the novel phenomena[8] and for constructing human governance of societies based not on totalitarianism but on freedom.

Service functions of many new kinds must expand, spread, and diversify to be able to satisfy intangible needs, some of which are not even known today. A large proportion of intangible needs are concerned with human relations. For example, there will be a growing need for the generation of integrative, cross-catalytic 'brain-circuits' of global human consciousness and global interaction: just the sort of activity that has taken place at this conference.

References

1. Malaska, P., 'Nature-Oriented Technology', Proceedings of WFSF XI World Conference in Budapest. London: Tycooly Pub., 1990

2. Cf. Reijo Wilenius, *Man Nature and Technology*. Jyväskylä: Ateena, 1987, in Finnish; and Daniel Bell, *The Coming of Post-Industrial Society: A Venture in Social Forecasting*. New York: Basic Books, 1975. Bell divides society into social structure, polity and culture, each ruled by an 'axial principle', which differs in various parts of the world.

3. Allen, Peter M., 'Towards a New Science of Complex Systems', in *Managing Global Issues: Reasons for Encouragement*, Proceedings of the Club of Rome Conference in Helsinki. Helsinki: Helsinki University, Lahti Research Center, 1984. Ervin Laszlo, 'The Crucial Epoch; Essential Knowledge for Living in a World in Transformation', *Futures*, Vol. 1 (Feb. 1984) and *Evolution: A Grand Synthesis*, New Science Library, 1987. G. Nicholis and Ilya Prigogine, *Self-Organization in Nonequilibrium Systems*. New York: John Wiley, 1977. Ilya Prigogine, *From Being to Becoming*. San Francisco: W.H. Freeman, 1980. Jean Voge, 'The Political Economy of Complexity: From the Information Economy to the "Complexity" Economy', *Information Economics and Policy*. North Holland: Co. Libraries Unlimited, 1983

4. Laszlo, Ervin, 'The Crucial Epoch', op.cit.

5. Lipton, Michael, *Why Poor People Stay Poor: Urban Bias in World Development*. Cambridge, MA: Harvard University Press, 1976

6. Bell, Daniel, op.cit., and Yoneji Masuda, *The Information Society as Post-Industrial Society*. Tokyo: Institute for the Information Society, 1980

7. Aulin, Arvid, *The Cybenetic Laws of Social Progress*. Oxford: Pergamon Press, 1982

8. See, for example: Club of Rome, 'Complexities: Scientific Seminar', in *Managing Global Issues: Reasons for Encouragement*, op.cit. Ilya Prigogine, *From Being to Becoming*, op. cit. Millan Zeleny, *Spontaneous Social Orders in the Science and Paxis of Complexity*. Tokyo: UN University, 1984. L.O. Chua, Editorial in the *International Journal of Bifurcation and Chaos*, vol. 1, 1, March 1991

Pentti Malaska has been a professor of management science and operations research at the Turku School of Economics and Business Administration (Finland) since 1966. He is a member of The Club of Rome and has been Secretary-General of the World Futures Studies Federation since 1990.

GLOBAL SOCIETY, GLOBAL PROBLEMS AND NEW FORMATS OF GLOBAL DECISION-MAKING

Miriam L. Campanella

I

The Kantian or post-Kantian notion of a global society
From an analytical and scholarly point of view, the terms 'world society' and 'global society' belong to the study of international relations or world politics. In the specialized language of these fields, the terms are intended to denote an idealistic cosmopolitan and universal society that includes all the peoples living on earth, without regard to cultural and ethical beliefs. However, in contrast to the long-established interpretation of the realist school, the Kantian theory of world order actually includes more institutional and realist features than generally acknowledged. For example, the notion of 'perpetual peace' did not aim to abolish the nation-state and national frontiers. According to a new and non-partisan interpretation of Kant's theory of world order, the Kantian core project of the global society is institutional and not merely ethical. The confederation of states to which he consecrated his institutional effort is very much like the Society of Nations or, more recently, the UN Security Council. For example:

> it is necessary to establish a federation of peoples (*Voerbund*) in accordance with the idea of the original social contract, so that the state will protect one another against external aggression while refraining from interference in one another's internal disagreements. And [. . .] this association (*Verbindung*) must not embody a sovereign power as in a civil constitution, but only a partnership (*Genossenschaft*) or confederation (*Foederalitaet*).[1]

Kant is insistent that this union of several states designed to preserve the peace, which may be called a permanent congress of states, is a 'voluntary gathering of various states which can be dissolved at any time, not an indissoluble association'.

In contrast, if one is to consider the idealistic limit of the Kantian view, the global society can be conceived of as an association of nation-states that are free to share or not to share common values and rules of behaviour, because of their intrinsic capability to associate for common well-being. Kant believed very strongly 'in the moral unity of mankind and in the existence of a global ethical commonwealth'. This was not a 'juridico-civil condition', that is 'the relation of men to each other in which they all alike stand socially under public coercive laws'.

The global society is an ethico-civil state [in which] they (peoples and states) are united under non-coercive laws, that is, *laws of virtue* alone. Further, because the duties of virtue apply to the entire human race, the concept of an ethical commonwealth is extended ideally to the whole of mankind.[1]

This presumption of universality is 'problematic', among other reasons because the historical variability of moral beliefs puts strict limits on the application of generous imperatives. In addition, the Kantian global society is not based solely on universal moral laws, but also on the duty to maintain the conditions within which commerce and peaceful intercourse between people are possible. However, it is also true that trade and economic interdependence cannot be understood only as peaceful intercourse. The conditions of 'universal hospitality' are often threatened by state protectionism of domestic markets. In other words, with a good empirical intuition, Kant recognized the reality of this global society in the trade and economic interdependence that existed between states and in the transnational ties between individuals, but was mistaken about the harmonious nature of these relations. The core Kantian idea of interdependence overlaps with that of harmony, and is the key concept in the liberal economic thought of the epoch.

Furthermore, Kant believed strongly in the self-realizing concept of global society. For him the global society is a society where 'the peoples of the earth have [. . .] entered in varying degrees into a universal community, and it has developed to the point where a violation of rights in one part of the world is felt everywhere'.[1]

This definition epitomizes what in technical terms is labelled the Kantian holistic-idealistic concept of a global society, and all the limits that have hampered the introduction of the concept in the theory and practice of international politics.

However, this is not a good reason – as the realist school has often maintained – to abandon the notion of global society. Rather the evolution of the world system from Kant's time to the present has paradoxically reconfirmed certain intuitions of Kantian political theory. The growth of global interdependences and transnational relations among peoples, individuals, groups, and so on, has occurred in the fields of economics, finance and communication, but has not developed to a great extent in ethical matters. The coming of a global society is no longer a matter of dreams, but is a concrete and challenging reality. Of course, the price to pay is the abandonment of the key concept of the Kantian paradigm, that of harmony. The coming global society calls for skilled management and governance of resources in order to face the pressures of conflicting interests to which the growth of interdependence has given rise.

II

A post-Kantian paradigm of the global society

Today's global society consists of conflicting social systems, and its future is not of a harmonious and self-realizing design. The global society in which we live is a highly complex and dynamic state of the world, in which regressive, self-destructive trends and unpredictable events occur, and in which all parts evolve irreversibly. From an analytical perspective, the frameworks that help us understand the confusing and complex reality of our increasingly global society are:

1   The pluralistic approach to the study of international affairs, in particular that of the Chicago school;
2   The efforts by scholars to consider the nature of power and conflict in the coming global society; and
3   The theory of decision that enables us to solve problems or to bring them under control.

In the post-Kantian paradigm of a global society, the actors form either non-territorial or territorial units such as nation-states, confederations of states or regional communities like that formed by the EEC.

The entrance of the non-territorial associations was first noted in 1945. In a chapter entitled 'The Interrelations of Political Associations' in *Systematic Politics*, Charles E. Merriam (the leader of the Chicago school) gave the first contemporary sketch of the new 'international' scene.[2] In his view, nation-states are only one class of associations that can be related to each other and to various sub-, trans-, and supranational associations. Many other legal and illegal associations act in economics, in scientific communities, in cultural and artistic groups, in criminal organizations, and so on. Because of this new 'population' of associations, he suggested changing the label of the traditional discipline of international relations to that of 'world politics'. For Merriam and his colleagues of the Chicago school, the task was the pluralistic study of whatever groups participated in the political process. In contrast to the European tradition that limited the study of foreign politics to states, governments, public law and institutions, the new approach expanded the traditional research field to include policies, groups, process, power and decision-making.[3] As far as world politics is concerned, the new approach considered the world scene as one populated by many associations (groups of interests, institutions, policies, and so on) that were interdependent and competitive in their scope and goals. This approach contrasts with the traditional school, which assumed the world scene to be one of a perennial state of threat and war, and the nation-state to be a unity acting for the whole national interest, including that of the corporations. Realist scholars maintain firmly that only a power-oriented approach can accurately describe the nature of international interactions, and that the role of non-territorial actors, and the new interdependences among state-actors, have not changed the very nature of international politics. The building of a global society is still to be properly conceived before it can be introduced into world affairs. The questions are always the same. Have the relations and the behaviour among national states really changed? What role do co-operation and co-ordination play? What about hegemony and leadership?

Keohane and Nye try to respond to some of these questions with their theory of 'complex interdependence'.[4] They argue that interdependence generates a hierarchy deficit. The hierarchy deficit affects both the ability of the state to set up a ranking of priority in domestic politics, and the ability of actors in the international arena to set up a ranking of powers. The first loss of ranking is due mainly to the long-term development of the welfare state in the advanced industrial countries. This has hampered national governments in arranging a strategic list of goals, and contrasts with the power-oriented policies of the nineteenth century and the first half of this century. The nation-states of the western countries, and the post-communist states now forming in Eastern Europe, are giving great scope to the multiplicity and conflicting goals of economic welfare. However, welfare policies and welfare departments are being challenged by new policy-making strategies in the area of government; evidence to this effect is coming from foreign trade departments. Their strategic role is growing, and their policies are gaining ground in foreign policy-making. But perhaps there is another way for the nation-state to maintain its power prerogatives: perhaps it could mask its prerogatives in the new policies of interdependence, or is yet another political evolution of the nation-state possible?

In order to answer the question of whether the trends towards a global society are effective or only ephemeral, it is necessary to understand whether the process of complex interdependence is part of the process of globalization. It is also necessary to understand whether globalization implies the decline of the nation-state. A crucial question to explore is how the nation-state is or is not adapting to the new evolutionary environment.

III

Globalization and the nation-state: a counter-intuitive perspective
After World War II, under the leadership of the US economy, a process of economic interdependence increasingly linked the national economies of the West. The growth of economic integration between the market-oriented economies was reputedly the main barrier against the centrally planned, state economies of the communist countries. The safeguarding of the 'free world' was placed in the hands of private entrepreneurs, and the role of governments was to act as facilitators of enterprises and ventures. However, since the 1950s, the formation of a world economy has been perceived as paradoxically weakening the role of the nation-state and strengthening regional economic integration. Theodor Geiger depicted a scenario of a future international system where the international economy is characterized by 'tensions between obtaining the benefits of international interdependence and preserving those of national freedom of action in both internal and external affairs'.[5] Forty-five years later, Robert Gilpin described the international economy in similar terms. In his major work, *The Political Economy of International Relations*, Gilpin notes that 'the clash between the integrating forces of the world economy and the centrifugal forces of the sovereign state has become one of the critical issues in contemporary international relations'.[6]

In recent years, alarm at the changing world order has been expressed by many analysts who fear an American decline. It is not surprising that the emerging global economy is seen as a challenge to the hegemonic role of the US economy since World War II. A first significant development is the expanding integration of the economies of the United States and Japan. The integration of the two economies in trade, finance, and production has 'initiated a vicious cycle of budget deficits, negative capital flows and trade imbalance that is deindustrializing America'.[7]

A second significant development is the rapid geographic shift in the focus of world industrial and economic activity. The uneven growth of national economies has caused the centre of the world economy to shift from the Atlantic to the Pacific Basin. With the meteoric rise of Japan and the Asian economies, the United States and Europe (both east and west) have suffered a relative decline. The continuing industrialization of Brazil, China and other developing countries has also begun to alter the international division of labour.[6] In addition, the leading sectors of the past half century (automobiles, consumer durables and so on) are no longer the major sources of growth and employment – at least, not in advanced economies. These industries are slowly being displaced by services, biotechnology and information industries, which are part of the post-industrial economy. The transition from 'energy-intensive' to 'knowledge-intensive' industries is reputedly the main cause of decline in western, North American and European economies. However, the shift of the centre from the western to East Asian countries has been exaggerated and misinterpreted. According to a naive modernization theory, which sees the beginning of modernization in the discovery of the American continent by Columbus, any shift from an old centre to another centre is interpreted as a sign of the decline of the old area. Among many other factors, what has really changed is the fact that the world is not only highly unstable, but also lacks a centre.

Given that the globalization process is no longer believed to have improved the international system, the difference between the 'global society' approach to the international system and the traditional realist approach had diminished. Now, the differences may be more those of semantics than of fundamentals. The problem is no longer whether or not 'global society' has a realistic or idealistic status, but rather, whether we are able to manage a global society or not. It is also a question of which institutional and non-institutional tools are available to us. Among other relevant questions is whether the nation-state is a useful tool for managing a global society, or simply an obstacle to it.

IV

The transformation of nation-state from geopolitical actor to geo-economic actor

Although evidence shows that the process of globalization does not eliminate the nation-state as an important actor, the very nature of the state is changing in an unpredictable way. The internal hierarchy of the central institutions of the state is under pressure to change. Transgovernmental relations have grown constantly in the past three decades, and are 'becoming an increasingly crucial part of every nation's external profile'.[8] The traditional monopoly of the foreign ministry on external contacts is challenged by non-governmental actors and by centralized and decentralized state agencies. In EEC countries, regional governments and sub-regional units have assumed a political profile in external contacts within the boundaries of the European Community.

In eastern countries, the changes that quickly developed between 1988 and 1990 are removing obstacles to economic expansion. The unification of Germany, the integration of Europe, the possibility of extending the EEC to eastern and to Middle Eastern countries, the resurgence of 'sub-nationalist trends' in the old and mature democracies as well as in the post-communist or new democracies of Europe: these factors are rapidly creating new actors and new decision-makers who are competing, conflicting and co-operating in world affairs.

As Edward Luttwak wrote in the summer of 1990, 'methods of commerce are displacing military methods – with disposable capital in lieu of military–technical advancement, and market penetration in lieu of garrisons and bases. But these are all tools, not purposes; what purposes will they serve?'[9] They will serve to compete or to co-operate in world business; and competitively or co-operatively, the action on all sides will always unfold without regard to frontiers, as Luttwak asserts.

In spite of the primacy of economics, the pressure to create alternatives and to choose among them falls back on politics once more. The government is charged not only with strategic decision-making and policy formulation, but also with the performance of these tasks through co-ordination and integration with other organizations and governments. Most often, governments make strategic decisions and long-term choices as member-states of a supranational community, for example the EEC.

V

Sensitivity, vulnerability and the crisis situation

Although the Kantian paradigm of global society did not ignore the concept of power, it certainly did not pay much attention to the notions of discord and conflict. A post-Kantian paradigm cannot afford to ignore such matters. Although military strength is no longer the main source of power in world affairs,[10] the concept of power is still important in the world community. Under conditions of interdependence, power has assumed more discreet forms and is more evenly distributed among international actors. Its manifest presence can nevertheless be detected by two measurable parameters: sensitivity and vulnerability. According to the Keohane and Nye definition, 'sensitivity involves degrees of responsiveness within a policy framework'.[4] 'Sensitivity' implies the question: 'How quickly do changes in one country bring costly changes in another, and how great are the costly effects?' A pertinent example of sensitivity is the responsiveness of OECD countries to the increased price of oil in 1971, 1973–4, and summer and autumn of 1990. In these circumstances, sensitivity means liability to costly effects. By contrast, 'vulnerability' denotes liability to suffer costs imposed by external events even after policies have been altered. As Prof. Soedjamoto of the UN University of Tokyo has so aptly stated:

> In the process of interdependence, we have all become vulnerable. Our societies are permeable to decisions taken elsewhere in the world. The dynamics of interdependence might be better understood if we think of the globe not in terms of a map of nations but as a meteorological map, where weather systems swirl independently of any national boundaries and low and high fronts create new climatic conditions far ahead of them.[11]

With regard to the capacity to make decisions, vulnerability produces deeper effects than sensitivity. The policies adopted by the vulnerable are ineffective in mitigating the actions of others. This is the case in Italy's relationship with France. This difference is important in understanding the impact of increases in oil prices: sensitivity in some OECD countries but vulnerability in others, as well as in many less-developed countries. However, vulnerability and sensitivity are not the only index of power relations. When different countries have to cope with the effects of sensitivity and vulnerability, then a crisis situation or, alternatively, a co-operative situation can evolve.

Sensitivity and vulnerability generate:

1 Co-operation (and co-ordination) if incremental policies adjust and adapt to other strategies.
2 Discord if decremental policies (resorting to basic imperatives) interact with other policies.
3 Crisis if strategic economic and political issues coalesce, inhibiting goal attainment. The Gulf Crisis shows impressive evidence of crisis-situation effects 2 and 3. Nowhere is interdependence so obvious as it is in international economics, and nowhere is it so sensitive and vulnerable as in world order. A crisis situation is present when sensitivity and vulnerability provoke a coalescence of different issues and produce the constraints of a threat to goal attainment.

Evidence for such an effect can be found in the Stock Exchange index throughout the Gulf Crisis. The Stock Exchange is the barometer of financial business. But the behaviour of the Stock Exchange also provides strong evidence for the coalescence of economics and politics, as well as of local and global links (interdependence), for global crisis seems to follow the pattern of Stock Exchange prices.

The following points can now be made:

1 The coalescence of economics/politics occurs when few selected strategic factors are involved;
2 The coalescence of local/global occurs when strategic areas are involved;
3 The crisis reaches the highest point when confusion among economics/ politics and local/global is greatest and when:
4 The decision of one actor is perceived by others as an intolerable challenge or threat to their own identity or to their position in the *status quo ante*.

A regional problem, the invasion of Kuwait, evolved rapidly, almost instantly (in terms of political units of time) into a 'global problem' because of the presence of all four of the above factors. US Secretary of State James Baker rebuffed the suggestion that the Iraqi invasion of Kuwait was an Arab issue for Arab states to settle. 'No,' he said, 'it is a world issue.' According to many news commentators, Iraqi aggression was a 'global crisis' of the first level. In the early days of the invasion, Flora Lewis provided a vivid and powerful description:

> The Arab regimes in the area are in imminent danger, which is why they welcome Western protective force. But America would lose not only its world power status but also its ability to govern its own destiny if it were unwilling to confront the menace. [. . .] The choice is not whether to confront Saddam Hussein or to seek a tolerable compromise, it is whether to accept the challenge now or later, in much worse circumstances (*International Herald Tribune* August 22, 1990).

Evidence of the difficulties in stating a comprehensive understanding of factors 1–3 above is present in the debate over the 'true' interests involved in the Gulf Crisis.

What is the true interest of the international community in the Gulf Crisis? Is it to ensure that the Gulf is the secure and stable source of reasonably priced oil for the industrialized West? Or is it to ensure that legal and political world order may be restored against the Iraqi aggression? On the pages of *The International Herald Tribune*, both theses have been strongly supported. The first was argued by Zbigniew Brzezinski as follows:

> The Iraqi aggression against Kuwait [. . .] portended nothing less than the subordination of the Gulf states to a power of demonstrated ruthlessness and radical orientation. Had the United States failed to respond immediately – as it did – it is very likely that Iraq would have emerged as the region's dominant power and the preponderant arbiter of the price of oil.

Developing his thesis, Brzezinski introduces the Carter Doctrine, that is to say, the geopolitical interest of the US in the Gulf. He sustains the idea that US intervention in the Gulf aims to prevent 'any hostile domination in the Gulf'. Another example of this policy is the decision for US naval intervention in summer 1987, during the Iraq–Iran war. For Brzezinski, 'President George Bush thus (1990) acted wisely, and in keeping with established American geostrategy, when he decided last week to deploy American forces to deter any further Iraqi moves, thereby credibly reassuring Saudi Arabia and the other Gulf states of American willingness to become militarily engaged even alone'.

On the other hand, for Charles Krauthammer, the issue in the Persian Gulf is 'world order, not just oil supply'. His commentary develops the following thesis:

> With the abdication of Soviet power, the world has been transformed from a bipolar into a unipolar one. The United States and the alliance it leads have unprecedented control of the international order – an order whose benignity and humanity have been testified to yet again by the rush of the newly liberated peoples of Eastern Europe to join.

The global nature of the Gulf Crisis rests on the fact that, under conditions of strong interdependence, it is impossible to isolate the economic level from the political level, national economic gain from international economics, and national interest from international economics. This central issue must be clearly understood before analytical distinctions are used to handle global issues.

VI

Global problems and global society

The growth of interdependence and complexity in the world system has increased dramatically, and the globalization issue has come to the attention not only of scholars and politicians, but also of the public.

Global problems and globalization are not only the new topics with which analysts of world affairs are concerned, but are becoming the new issues that are challenging both developed and less-developed countries. We can say about globalization what Kenneth Boulding wrote about complexity: globalization cannot be identified with goodness, because globalization (just like increasing complexity) can be perverse and could even lead to extinction.[12] It is not paradoxical to argue that obstacles to the evolution of a world or global society arise from the speed and magnitude of global dynamics.

It is noteworthy that we address the issue of globalization under the expression 'global problems'. We perceive the process of the globalization of our world as a long list of problems to solve. And we conceive of a problem as a situation that diverges significantly from what is considered to be a desirable state of affairs. It is not surprising that globalization is perceived in a rather negative way; one reason for this is that global problems are of the kind that no single national society is able to cope with or to simply take under its own control.

We have seen that the solution to global problems depends on many factors, and that it required a great deal of co-operation and co-ordination among actors. These are conditions that have been only poorly understood in the climate of competition among nation-states, jealous of their prerogatives, and in a time of nuclear confrontation between the two 'super-powers'.

A further base for the generation of negative attitudes toward globalization is the perceived threat it poses to community values and cultural identities. The growth of complexity (in terms of the number of actors in a given situation) inhibits the mechanism of social adaptability and the working of integrating procedures. These procedures require very specific conditions for their functioning, including locally stable states, and large amounts of time. These two integrating conditions are dramatically lacking in the never-ending dynamics of globalization. There is no locally stable state because interdependence embraces only part of the world and there is pressure of time due to simultaneity or the *contagion effect*[13] produced by the diffusion of life-styles dependent on high-technology.

For the time being, there are two options: the option to build up the conditions of a global society, and the option to regress towards a more fragmented society (more fragmented than the past world of nation-states). Visualizing the problems in a practical way and placing them on an agenda depends on our capacity to decide which paradigm of global modernization we must select. This implies that we have to modify our attitudes towards the management of government, because as Michael Kirby states:

1　The major challenges facing governments have become both technical and extremely complex. They are difficult to solve since in many cases publicly acceptable 'solutions' may not exist.
2　Many citizens do not believe that there is such a thing as a problem for which the government cannot find a solution that does not cause them pain personally [. . .] The governance problem is caused therefore in part by the nature of the problems the governments face, in part by the failure of the governing and the governed to reach a consensus on what constitutes reality and hence on what is truly possible.[11]

However, the link between globalization and global society is not deterministic. It is not true that more globalization implies a more global society. Between globalization and the global society there are global problems. We define global problems as those requiring co-ordination and implementation of decisions in ways that go beyond the boundaries and capabilities of any single actor or decision-maker.

In regard to problem solution, global issues belong to the category of 'ill-structured problems' or 'complex problems'. They are phenomena that do not admit of a single definitive formulation, let alone a single exact solution.[14] The essence of global phenomena cannot be fully captured by any single scheme. Unlike well-structured problems, whose definition and solution are presumably the same for all experts, the definition and solution of ill-structured problems are variable for each interested party. For this reason alone, they cannot be resolved by such simple decision mechanisms as 'widespread consensus'.

Once again, we need different ways of thinking about such issues if we are even to grasp the true nature of their complexity. The following four aspects characterize the nature of global problems:[15]

1　Global problems arise from local issues, and require global decision
2　Global decision needs local implementation
3　Local implementation depends on global behaviour
4　Local implementation depends on global decision.

This oversimplified representation of a global problem shows that the boomerang effect pervades the status of global problems. How is this boomerang effect brought under control? What kind of logic is required?

The boomerang effect is the non-linear process that occurs given conditions of interdependence. In seeking goals in an interdependent environment, strategic actors amplify their decision-making process, and thereby activate latent potential actors, attracting them to the decision-making process. The net result is an amplification–feedback loop that counteracts or complicates conventional dynamics (with top-down lines of command) by weakening the capacity to achieve goals and objectives in the given environment.

In an empirical way, the solution to each strategic problem depends upon the sum of behaviours of all the actual (and potential) actors involved in the problem and attracted to the decision-making process. But this requires a return to the initial decision.

From these counter-revolutionary dynamics one of the main features of globalization is derived: globalization is not a particular and definite class of phenomena. Globalization is the way in which problems are considered under particular conditions. Problems are global when they cannot be resolved within the boundary of a single unit of command-taking, decision-making, or system-operation.

For the moment, we can only adopt 'negative learning'[16] in order to avoid some traps, such as:

– treating one symptom in isolation, thereby exacerbating others;
– seeking short-term, politically expedient solutions, which lead to long-term degradation and a considerable worsening of the problem;
– intervening in the socio-economic system at precisely those points where intervention is ineffective in the medium to long term, but is politically effective in the short term;
– devising solutions based on static analysis of a problem, whereas the dynamic time-dependent elements are by far the most important.

But the question still remains: what are the ways to handle global problems?

References
1. Hurrell, Andrew, 'Kant and the Kantian Paradigm in International Relations', in *Review of International Studies* No. 106, pp. 183–205, 1990
2. Merriam, Charles E., *Systematic Politics*. Chicago: University of Chicago Press, 1949

3. Fox, William T. R., 'Pluralism, The Science of Politics, and the World System', in *World Politics*, Vol. XXii, No. 4, pp. 597–611, 1975

4. Keohane, Robert and Joseph Nye, *Power and Interdependence. World Politics in Transition*. Boston: Little Brown and Company, 1977

5. Geiger, Theodor (translation), *The Future of the International System: the United States and the World Political Economy*. Boston: Allen and Unwin, 1988

6. Gilpin, Robert, *The Political Economy of International Relations*. Princeton: Princeton University Press, 1987

7. Calder, Kent, 'The Emerging Politics of the Trans-Pacific Economy' in *World Politics Journal* No. 2, pp. 593–623, 1985

8. Karvonen, Lauri and Bengt Sundelius, 'Interdependence and Foreign Policy Management in Sweden and Finland' in *International Studies Quarterly*, Vol. 34 No. 2, June 1990

9. Luttwak, Edward, 'From Geopolitics to Geo-Economics', in *The National Interest*, No. 20, pp. 17–23, 1990

10. Hoffman, Stanley, *Duties Beyond Borders*. Syracuse: Syracuse University Press, 1981

11. Kirby, Michael J. L., 'Complexity, Democracy and Governance', in *The Science and Praxis of Complexity*, Contribution to the Symposium held at Montpellier, 9–11 May, 1984. Tokyo: The United Nations University, 1985

12. Boulding, Kenneth, The Limits to Societal Growth in A. H. Hawley (ed.) *Societal Growth, Processes and Implications*. New York: The Free Press, 1979

13. Rosenau, James, *Change, Peace and Scholarship*, mimeo ISA London, 1989

14. Weick, Karl E., *The Social Psychology of Organizing*. New York: Random House, 1979

15. Campanella, Miriam L., 'Globalization: Processes and Interpretations' in *World Futures*, Vol. 30, pp. 1–16, 1990

16. Modelski, George, 'Is World Politics Evolutionary Learning?' in *International Organization*, Vol. 44, No. 1, pp. 1–24, 1990

Miriam L. Campanella is a senior researcher at the Department of Social Sciences at the University of Turin and a Fellow at the Center for International Relations at Massachusetts Institute of Technology, Cambridge, US.

PART 2

MANAGEMENT OF THE TRANSITION: THE ROLE OF PUBLIC AND PRIVATE SECTORS

PEACEFUL DISINTEGRATION OF THE SOVIET TOTALITARIAN EMPIRE AS A NECESSARY PRECONDITION FOR THE TRANSITION TO GLOBAL SOCIETY

Volodymyr Vassilenko

I

The present stage of history is often called the period of transition to a global society. During this period, humankind has to build a new social world order and, to do this, public institutions, principally governmental ones, have to be used. It is absolutely necessary to establish peaceful relations between states, and to involve all of them in finding solutions to present and future local, regional and global problems, thereby creating the preconditions necessary for a stable and integrated global society.

An integrated global society has to secure close and friendly relations between different ethnic, national and cultural entities without discrimination and without destruction of the identity of each. 'Diversity in unity and unity in diversity' must be the basic principle of public governance within the framework of a future global society. Only unconditional compliance with this fundamental and universal principle of natural and social life will make possible the creation of a global society capable of securing social justice, solidarity, friendship, altruism, and respect for human rights and the dignity of all peoples.

When searching for ways to achieve a global society, one must remember that more than seventy years ago, the communists who came to power in the Russian Empire tried to start building a communist global society with the same laudable aims. This attempt, however, was a complete failure because of the very nature of communist ideology and practice. Lenin's and Stalin's interpretation of this ideology resulted in a horrible mixture of Marxist theory, Nietzschean ideology and Greater Russian chauvinistic, imperialistic thinking.

The main communist ideological postulates based on original Marxist doctrine were the following:

1 Abolition of private ownership, which was seen as the main source of exploitation and all social ills throughout the world, and the legislation of only one form of ownership, namely state ownership.
2 Negation of the market economy, based on different forms of ownership, and the introduction of a centrally directed, state-planned economy, based on state ownership.
3 Recognition of the proletariat as the predominant social force, and the creation of the proletarian state as an instrument for the suppression of the bourgeoisie and petty-bourgeoisie classes of society.
4 Recognition of the communist party as the proletarian party, thus the only ruling political party; and the prohibition of all other political parties, and of independent social organizations and movements.
5 Proclamation of communist ideology as the only valid and true teaching, and declaration of merciless war against other social, philosophical and spiritual doctrines, particularly religion.
6 Proclamation of the primacy of proletarian class values over universal human values, and the precedence of ideology and policy over law.
7 Denial of the distinction between peoples for the sake of proletarian solidarity and unity, and proclamation of the inevitability and necessity for all peoples to merge into a world communist state – homogeneous, classless and nationless.

The communist ideological postulates based on Nietzschean ideology and Greater Russian chauvinistic, imperialistic thinking were the following:

1 The creation of a superior type of human being with new consciousness and morals who would be fit for the future communist society, and who can be compared with the Nietzschean romantic ideal of the 'superman'.
2 The formation of a world proletarian state with Russia as its nucleus and champion of permanent communist revolution, involving all other countries of the globe.

According to the above-mentioned ideological postulates, the ultimate goal of the communist movement, which was especially strong in the Russian Empire, consisted of winning state power and creating a world proletarian state capable of abolishing private ownership and securing social justice for all.

II

After the October 1917 revolution, the Russian Empire collapsed and disintegrated into several nation-states. Some of them, for example, Poland,

Finland, Latvia, Estonia and Lithuania, joined the western world. Others, such as the Russian Federation, Ukraine, Belorussia and the Transcaucasian states, became independent Soviet socialist republics. For prompt achievement of communist goals, the latter joined together as the Union of Soviet Socialist Republics (USSR) by signing the Union Treaty in 1922.

The formation of the Union of Soviet Socialist Republics was considered a first step towards the future world communist state and a vanguard for the continuation of the socialist revolution on a worldwide scale. But neither permanent revolution nor a world communist state came into being. The socialist revolution did not spread beyond the borders of the USSR. Instead of the promised world proletarian state, a totalitarian state was established on one-sixth of the surface of the planet. Despite the aspirations of the peoples of the republics within the Union, Stalin quickly converted the Union of Republics into a single, monolithic state, although under Soviet constitutional law, the USSR remained a federation.

State ownership became virtually the only form of ownership, excluding all other forms including private ownership. Peasants were deprived of their land and driven onto collective farms. The state governed all, and a highly centralized economic system was established. Political parties were prohibited, except the Communist Party of the Soviet Union (CPSU). The higher organs of the CPSU misappropriated the functions of the state, and became the only guiding and decision-making forces in all spheres of political, economic, social and cultural life. Freedom of the press was suppressed. Marxism-Leninism was declared to be the official doctrine of the CPSU. CPSU ideologists invented the 'nations merger' theory, according to which the different nations of the USSR would become a single ethnic entity, namely the 'Soviet people'. This theory became the basis for the creation of a new human species, '*Homo sovietiqus*', deprived of historical memory, national consciousness, traditions, religion, customs, language and culture.

Any attempt to protest, or even to show dissatisfaction, was severely punished. But even repression could not save the communist model from complete failure. The general reason for the failure was that the ways and means of achieving social aims contradicted objective and universal fundamentals, such as the principles of diversity and competition in the forms of natural and social life, natural selection, and people's development in freedom.

The errors of the communist model were not due to its basic aims of social justice, solidarity, altruism and friendship but rather to the attempts to put the model into practice by ignoring fundamental and universal principles. The stubborn refusal of the communist regimes in various countries to comply with these principles led to the denial of human freedom, and to monopolization and enforced uniformity in all spheres of life. Thus the creative abilities and activities of nations and individuals were considerably diminished. This is the real and underlying reason for the collapse of the communist system in Eastern Europe and for the disintegration of the USSR that we are witnessing today.

The systemic crisis obliged the CPSU leadership to introduce *perestroika* (rebuilding) of existing political, economic and governmental structures. As a result, from 1985 the USSR was in a state of transition. There are three main complementary elements to the transition of the framework of the USSR:

1 From repression and neglect of human and civil rights to a democratic, civil society.
2 From a centrally planned economy to a market economy.
3 From a highly centralized, totalitarian empire to a loose community of sovereign states governed by the rule of law.

The most important common concern of all progressive political forces in the former USSR is to secure human and civil rights and to build an open, democratic society. The legislative bodies in the republics have already adopted several laws that, with due regard to existing international standards, guarantee greater freedom and rights for individuals. This process is not easy and is far from complete. Nevertheless, the laws already adopted establish multi-party political systems, guarantee freedom of the press and recognize different forms of property ownership, including private ownership.

These first steps have created the primary conditions for democratic social development and for the emergence of a market economy in the republics of the former USSR. They will, of course, be confronted with great difficulties on the way to a market economy. Centralized government and central planning have left every republic with a distorted and ruined economy, full of bankrupt monopolies: on the one hand, beset by shortages and corruption, and on the other, lacking its own external economic infrastructure. In addition, until recently, the Soviet legal system did not even provide or promote the proper conditions for foreign business activities on USSR territory.

The republics are trying to create a new basis for their economic systems by adopting laws on foreign economic relations, and to establish trade and other economic links with foreign countries as well as between themselves. It is now quite clear that, despite all the difficulties and obstacles, social life will be based on a multi-party system and a market economy.

The status and future fate of the republics is even more problematic. The status of the Soviet Union was frequently misunderstood in the West because it was often called Russia. In fact, the USSR was not Russia, neither was it a single nation-state. According to Soviet constitutional law, the USSR was a united multinational state, that is, a federation consisting of fifteen sovereign republics that were themselves nation-states. A particular feature of the USSR was that, since 1936, when the USSR Constitution of 1924 (based on the Union Treaty of 1922) was replaced by the so-called Stalin Constitution, the Federation became, to all intents and purposes, an overly centralized empire-state. That is why the USSR was often incorrectly called a colonial nation. The peoples of the republics were not oppressed by some other dominant nation; they were oppressed by central, cosmopolitan, bureaucratic structures. For decades, tremendous power had been accumulated by Communist Party leaders, and by the enormous and numerous union ministries that ignored the national interests of republics. All the different peoples, including Russians, suffered from this dictatorship. Thus, the real nature of the USSR empire was not colonial – it was totalitarian.

That empire has now crumbled. The republics, after liberating themselves from the central, totalitarian structures, want to develop mutually advantageous relations between themselves as sovereign states. Despite this long-held desire of the republics, expressed in their declarations of sovereignty, the Soviet leadership tried to preserve the so-called centre, the numerous central structures with huge armies of bureaucrats. Thus, for all practical purposes, the USSR tried to retain its totalitarian empire. To maintain centralization and dictatorship is, however, incompatible with the principles of democracy and self-determination. The most reasonable solution is the peaceful disintegration of the USSR and its restructure into a community of democratic, sovereign states, united on a voluntary basis.

Whatever their future may be, the republics have regained considerable power in the sphere of foreign relations, particularly in external economic relations. Even according to former constitutional provisions, every republic had the right to enter into relations with other states, conclude treaties with them, exchange diplomatic and consular representatives, and take part in the work of international organizations (Article 80 of the USSR Constitution).

Foreign states now have to solve the problem of relations with the republics of the former USSR. The republics are now entering a new stage of their historical development, the depth and scale of which is of paramount importance for European and world order. They are striving to build civil societies and to establish broad co-operation with all countries and peoples of the planet, and thus become an integral part of the future global society. The West could not continue to ignore the right and desire of the republics to participate directly in international relations. But western states and international institutions long preferred to deal with the USSR, fearing that direct relations with the republics would contribute to the breakdown of the USSR and thus create dangerous instability in Europe and the world. The underlying idea was and continues to be that the disintegration of the Soviet Union will be accompanied by violence that could lead to loss of central control over the USSR's vast nuclear arsenal. In one speech, Mikhail Gorbachev, exploiting this western idea, said that the whole world was afraid that if the republics became independent, fifteen nuclear states would emerge in the place of one. That was a crude argument, calculated to persuade western states to persist in refusing recognition to the republics as direct and sovereign participants in international relations, despite the clear provisions for this in the USSR Constitution.

In this connection, it is important to recognize that most acts of violence during the disintegration of the Soviet empire occurred only when the Union government oppressed national movements and the aspirations of the republics for independence. No republic has demanded nuclear weapons; on the contrary, some of them – for example Ukraine and Belorussia – have declared their intention to become nuclear-free states.

Events in the former Soviet Union are complicated and are moving so quickly that most western policy-makers cannot easily grasp their true meaning and significance. This is understandable. It is also natural that the West is anxious about is own security. What is less natural, and is even immoral, is that western states tried to secure their own interests at the expense of the freedom of the peoples of the former Soviet republics.

Such a stand was harmful and dangerous for the West itself. It is difficult to talk of democratic reforms, individual and collective freedom, and the protection of minorities, while simultaneously contributing to the preservation of totalitarianism by denying other nations their right to freedom of choice. The West's support of the Soviet totalitarian empire and the artificial exclusion of the republics from international co-operation created serious obstacles for the creation of a global society. This future global society must be united in freedom and find its security in the acknowledgement of universal human values.

Volodymyr Vassilenko is a professor at the Institute of Foreign Relations and International Law, Kiev State University. He is a specialist in the field of constitutional and public international law and has been the scientific adviser to the Ukrainian Ministry of Foreign Affairs for many years.

A NEW ETHIC
FOR THE PUBLIC SECTOR

Adamou Ndam Njoya

I

The human being at the heart of society

The global society is one of the great and incontrovertible realities of our time. But it is a reality that needs to be consolidated, for there are distinct limitations to what has become a watchword in international organizations and conferences about the co-operation and values shared by human beings regardless of frontiers. We stress the importance of the human being over and above national or territorial barriers, despite the inadequacies of national societies, and this is the first point I wish to make. Our lives and development still depend largely on states, institutions, officials and governments, the 'direct actors' in the international arena who are responsible for shaping international society and determining the stages of its evolution. These same entities are also 'indirect actors', as they preside over the creation of conditions enabling organizations and institutions, governmental or non-governmental, to operate effectively in the international sphere.

My second point, however, is that at the heart of every institution, be it domestic, national or international, stands the human being: the individual 'actor', the life and soul, working for or against the fulfilment of the institution's objectives. It is he or she who sustains the cogs and wheels of the institution, who is the deciding factor in the structures and institutions of government, in the management of other human beings and the administration of society, national or international. The significance of the human actor in all this is the basic reality that must be grasped if we are to understand the role of the public sector in the management of the transition to a global society. For particularities and individualities often exercise an all-important influence among both the governors – the administrators of society – and the governed.

Thirdly, there is today a marked acceleration in the process of consolidating world society as an effective entity, a genuine global community. New

Age thinking and growing environmental awareness are bringing about a dynamic shift in concepts and values, regardless of national or territorial boundaries. Acting as they do on behalf of human beings, governments are at the heart of all such developments.

Shifts of this nature often seem to happen when, faced with the damage wrought by humanity and some of its creations, people become profoundly aware of the need to work for the transformation of society. Whether our views are religious or otherwise, we can all find points of reference and expressions of values that play a decisive role in the life of the human being and in the building of society. This is something no government can afford to ignore.

II

The public sector as guardian of values

The public sector is, in effect, a crystallization of values at a given moment in time, when socializing human beings entrust the governance of their relations to a framework or mechanism. This they are compelled to do by the problems and realities of the environment, such as those now confronting us on the eve of the third millenium, and compelling us to consolidate the global society.

Why do we delegate this task to the public sector? Much of the answer lies in two human characteristics that are central to the management of society and therefore to the actions of governments during this phase of transition to a global society: these two characteristics are selfishness and generosity. The public sector is the 'actor' given the role of setting the terms of the contract, it is the consensus that emerges from among the membership of society. It represents a unifying factor between elements that are in conflict and those that complement one another, it acts as a catalyst for other institutions or individuals. But the public sector consists of human beings, who are its mainspring, and they are beset by their own selfishness and generosity as much as by their values and beliefs. All this is becoming increasingly significant in the consolidation phase of a global society, and should be borne in mind by those who govern.

The character and activities of the public sector are governed by the values and beliefs of the members of society. Personality and temperament are therefore as influential as the environmental and other problems facing those who govern; hence the fluctuations in the course of human history between openness towards others and isolationism. But at each stage, humanity has increased its awareness that the earth is like a 'Noah's ark', which suggests that there is a law of logic governing our evolution towards global thinking, with all the diversities of humankind as components of this law. The fragmentation caused by human particularities is gradually giving way to a coherent whole that expresses itself at different levels, culminating in the state or nation. Owing to negative developments in human values, however, these states or nations are becoming entrenched in the selfishness that characterizes individualities, giving rise to so-called 'localized' societies or states – meaning that they are closed, narrow, protective of their values, their resources, and above all of their nationals. This is happening despite progress towards a global society.

The essential task of the public sector is to defend the interests of the members of society, organizing not only internal affairs but relations with all that is external to the framework of the given society. The selfish instincts of the individualized human being, however, will often find expression at a higher level when those who bear direct responsibility are bent on serving nothing but their own interests. Indeed, history tells of a long list of monarchs and heads of state who have stirred up conflicts merely to satisfy personal ambitions. A case in point is the war that has recently wracked the Gulf, proving that the phenomenon is still very much with us and constitutes a current danger that must be combated unremittingly. Such attitudes place constraints upon the evolution and consolidation of the global society, but also serve to test the effectiveness of the machinery set in motion by this evolution. The mechanisms of intervention to remove obstacles along the path to a global society are a matter for the public sector to analyse, through national and international organizations. From this it will be possible to set standards of management in which the impact of human intervention will vary according to the qualities and deficiencies of those concerned, and to the degree that the global society places the emphasis on the human being.

III

Manifestations of global society and governments
The foundation of the League of Nations represented a notable stage in the manifestation of the global society as a structured and effective entity. However, it was to prove powerless when confronted with Mussolini's Fascists and Hitler's Nazis, and was able to prevent neither localized conflict nor escalation into world war, ultimately caused by individuals driven by personal ambition. Swept away by the war, this prototype organization was replaced by the United Nations, which found a proving ground in Korea and later in the difficult phase of decolonization. More recently the total unanimity within the UN in opposing Iraq's invasion of Kuwait, a sovereign

neighbour state, arguably represented the triumph of the global society. The same might be said of the construction and co-operation currently being organized in economic, social, cultural and humanitarian fields, especially that aimed at the developing or disaster-threatened countries. I need only cite the mechanisms of international co-operation developed by the UN since its inception, particularly the specialist institutions under the aegis of the Economic and Social Council (ECOSOC).

Human beings inspired by selfishness or generosity

Motivation for actions contributing to the strengthening of the global society is directly linked to the factor of internal order, which depends on human 'actors'. Human selfishness has given rise to the localized society or state, which is the product of negative exploitation of values by those who run the institutional machinery. In the name of a wide diversity of ideologies, barriers have been erected between human beings, and selfishness has been translated into armed conflict and war. Those ideologies that are racist, such as Nazism and Fascism, and in our own time apartheid in South Africa, have had especially appalling consequences in their destruction and degradation of the human being. These egocentric instincts still prevail in numerous countries, fostering concepts of rejection and exclusion, which constitute real threats to the harmonization of relations between peoples and the affirmation of a global society. Dehumanizing ideologies and actions, which strongly influenced the options available and the directions chosen after World War II towards establishing a global society, show that each step in the direction of that society is precarious and susceptible to human recalcitrance.

Although in our own epoch we see the breakdown of frontiers and barriers between peoples and between societies, many limitations remain. A wide variety of obstacles and impediments have been created by human beings as a result of the narrow interests that they favour, and pernicious new forms of resistance are springing up in many regions and countries of the world. Whilst levels of development make integration easy for the countries of the North, the situation is quite different for those of the South. The difficulties of running a state, and the malfunctioning of the public sector owing to inadequate mobilization of human and other resources, are delaying their rise to a level at which they can contribute effectively to the affirmation of a global society. Further difficulties will arise if more and more nationals from the North take over the running of countries in the South. Efficient banking and economic systems continue to elude the developing nations, especially in Africa, where the affairs of certain countries and sub-regions are as North-dominated as in the years of colonial rule. This is not in the interests of a global society. In order to change this state of affairs, responsibilities must be defined, and above all the countries of the South must work to create confidence.

We are at a point of transition in the current phase of the progression towards what we are calling a global society, that is the human community acting as one entity. It is as though humanity, recognizing that its defects have caused considerable destruction and loss of life and that certain hazards of its own making threaten its very existence, has become profoundly conscious of the earth's uniqueness and the inevitability of evolution towards a global society. This heightening of awareness is strengthened by technological advances, of which those in the field of communications are the most influential. Concerted action and systems of action are becoming the rule. Here again the public sector has the last word, even if the direct investors and actors are privately owned multinational companies.

IV

Management of new ways of being

Under the impact of progress in science and technology, changes in mentality, and the genesis of new ways of being, we are abandoning haphazard approaches to a global society in favour of a considered, organized and deliberate system. The League of Nations was an important step, but it was burdened with the legacy of the violence that reigned before its inception. The term 'league' was a product of World War I and was therefore of a purely arbitrary nature, though it was ostensibly the brainchild of a university professor turned President of the United States. To visit Princeton, to taste the atmosphere that prevails there and see how Woodrow Wilson lived, is to appreciate the orientations and characteristics that were imprinted upon the League of Nations.

This is another instance of the human factor intervening in the birth and life of public institutions. The League of Nations lacked an ethical basis. Once Woodrow Wilson had left office, the Americans withdrew into themselves and ignored the League of Nations. The localized society and localized state prevailed. The world, still recovering from a ruinous war, suffered the consequences. Italy, under Mussolini, invaded Ethiopia; other countries did nothing, the interests of their public institutions appearing to lie elsewhere. The League of Nations was soon submerged by Hitler and the Nazis, and by World War II. From its ashes rose the United Nations, again in accidental fashion but this time after lengthy deliberation in the light of recent experience. With the United Nations we enter the era of rejection of and resistance to all forms of violence. The global society, now establishing itself as a fully fledged and well-organized entity, starts to acquire the foundations of its humanity and therefore of its durability.

By reducing geographical spaces, science and technology have succeeded in reconciling peoples, breaking through political isolation, and penetrating the consciousness of both the governors and the governed, thereby dictating new attitudes. Yet there remains the phenomenon of particularities, of human identities, resulting in problems such as unwanted immigration, which is poisoning relations in both the North and the South, and must be appropriately addressed by all governments.

Another problem is that the institution of a State or an international organization has an abstract character, but is sustained by human 'actors'. Consequently the whims and particularities of the latter can divert the public sector from its primary function, as has been seen in certain countries; the public sector is often taken hostage by an ethnic or ideological group. While reflecting particularities, therefore, public institutions need to limit the negative influence and actions of certain individuals or groups.

Since World War II, we have experienced a period of constructive management and recognition of both the globality of human society and the need to create harmony in our world. Confirmation of this is found in efforts towards the management of the environment and the safeguarding of peace and human rights. This call for humanization is compelling states to be true managers of change, true protectors of the knowledge that leads to change and to begin to abandon the phenomenon of the localized, selfish, closed state. This is not easy, since it requires nothing short of a revolution whose achievements must be asserted in the face of human selfishness.

The situation is perhaps at its worst in Africa, where republics dedicated to peace and human rights should have been founded in the territories formerly under foreign domination, with unity of the entire continent as the final goal. Instead, individualities have prevailed and public institutions have served only to reinforce the phenomenon of localized states. Henceforth, however, the realities of evolution towards a global society will be inescapable. Societies can ensure their own durability and that of the global society only by creating the conditions for a permanently adaptable national base with a fresh perspective of openness towards others. This must then be translated into service beyond the localized framework, with a shift towards humanity and responsibility reflected in open, generous concepts of values rather than selfish ones leading to internal or international conflict.

Facilitating the encounter of human beings
The public sector, that is, those who govern, must orient thinking and acting towards this new ethic, on which activities at both internal and

international level can be based. But the development of a new ethic is fraught with difficulties because governments, as the guardians of given values, are required to preserve a consensus arrived at within a framework of political rivalry, involving individuals gathered around tendencies that frequently conflict. As public institutions, they must also face up to the actions of the people from whom they derive their legitimacy. These actions can give birth to new values, often leading to changes in the basis of the consensus; such was the experience of the eastern bloc countries, with *perestroika* and *glasnost* becoming the starting signal for action on a wider scale. These developments have now transcended the region and reached other continents including Africa.

Intervention by government institutions is needed for effective management of the environment and the preservation of the common heritage of mankind; and for management of peace and human rights according to international conventions, of which nations and states are the authors and principal guarantors. By monitoring activities in these fields and others requiring concerted action by the international community, one may classify governments according to their degree of perception and accomplishment; on an internal level at first, regarding the extent to which government institutions are involved, then at regional and sub-regional levels with regard to the effectiveness of a government's contribution to joint bodies.

In advancing towards the consolidation of a global society, governments must take account of basic factors and condition them for the better. Foremost among these factors are the need for a profound change in ways of being, thinking and acting, among individuals and societies. Tendencies to dominate must give way to humanization, encounters between human beings and between societies at their best level, to enable the best of global society to emerge. Only then will it be possible to set about reducing the phenomenon of localized states, of which there are so many examples throughout the world.

V

The fundamental task of governments

The task facing governments is to be custodians of essential resources, to confront the threat of external forces, organized or not, and to organize and manage international relations. This may be seen as a step towards establishing a human community in which a wealth of diverse identities can develop in enlightened and humanizing rivalry.

Efforts to evolve towards a global society in this way vary enormously from one country to another, one region to another. The real problem for all concerned is firstly to create and permanently maintain the conditions for dialogue, for exchanges, for trust between human beings and between societies; then to develop cultural, economic, technological and scientific capacities to satisfy physical, intellectual and spiritual needs; and finally, to strengthen awareness of identity, thereby consolidating trust and mutual respect. This involves the generation of dynamic internal forces with a real capacity for action. The result will be to create conditions of co-operation.

The dynamic of all human institutions, and more especially of public sector institutions which are responsible for organizing relations within and between societies, is the drive towards consensus. The consensus reached gives rise to the juridical basis of a given society, where every member has certain rights and duties. Where human beings are concerned, however, differences always emerge with change and lead to a different consensus, bringing the necessity for adjustments or the establishment of other juridical bases. For human beings, nothing is permanent; human creations are constantly bringing about environmental and behavioural change. There is thus a shift away from localized and selfish concepts of values and ways of thinking, towards open forms more in keeping with the evolution towards a global society, the richest expression of these realities.

The rules laid down by public institutions must be adapted accordingly; governments must assert themselves in their role as managers of change and promoters of change, and not as the guardians of a conservatism and maintenance of the status quo at all costs.

Governments and the stages of progress towards a global society
Realities both past and present testify to the logic of an evolution towards globalization whereby the regions of the world are gradually becoming components of world society. It is a long process in which a wide variety of factors have intervened, including oppression and war, and the defiance of hegemony or inhumanity. The success of efforts towards co-operation and integration in Europe after centuries of nationalistic governments offers a fine example of the triumph of unity in diversity. This contrasts with the failure of the socialist bloc, which tried to build its identity on foundations of a dominant, localized ideology.

Power may continue to play a decisive role, but can no longer constitute the means to build a global framework. This is illustrated by what happened in the Gulf: Iraqi ambitions, or at least the ambitions of the Iraqi president, encountered an immediate reaction of unqualified world-wide resistance. We are in another age, one that excludes force as a means of furthering national ambitions; force can only be counter-productive, as in the futile war between Iraq and Iran, which delayed regional development in that part of the world. In certain countries, however, it is still a brutal reality at local level; but international pressures now limit systematic exploitation, with the result that governments can no longer have entirely their own way. The global society is striving to exert its influence to the full.

Within international organizations, however, there is always the risk that a monopoly of leadership by the economic, financial and technological superpowers will limit the development of a global society to the predominance of the laws and opinions of the most powerful.

Obstacles to the creation of a global society will remain to a greater or lesser degree in different countries or regions of the world. Starting from a positive theoretical base, then, how can the obstacles be overcome? A network of co-operation must be created; and here the spiritual dimensions assume considerable importance owing to their impact on individuals and hence on the practical workings of systems of government.

VI

The necessity for a new ethic

Shifts towards the development of a world community cannot be durable and irreversible unless fundamental changes take place at the level of the values and concepts underlying governmental practice. In other words, localized or selfish values, the localized ethic, must give way to the new ethic.

At present, all change is brought about by localized actors working in localized frameworks of government, which are sustained by localized individuals obsessed with their own interests. This is because governments and states have either been developed by communities to translate given values into fact, or have been elaborated by elites who enjoy a monopoly of power and protect their vested interests at all costs.

Governments are considered above all to have as their purpose the maintenance of a framework of self-interest, and as being the organized reflection of the instinct for distrust of the unknown and the alien.

History teaches us that nations have frequently been the offspring of tensions resulting from the absorption of one group by another more powerful and dominant group. In many cases there have been cycles of resistance, war and revenge. The futility and the dehumanizing effect of war may now finally have been learned, but the co-operation and meeting of cultures which are the hallmark of progress towards a global society are still taking place in the context of a tradition of the pursuit of national self-interest. The distrust that colours relations in the global society will not be removed by the leading international organizations, which have a localized base because they are the products of states and regional groupings, and are often preoccupied with international protection of their domestic status quo.

Rapid developments in science and technology have contributed to a drastic reduction in the perceived dimensions of our world, and even seem to place the conquest of the universe within humanity's grasp. But governments that play an influential role in this work are often motivated by the associated concerns of military defence and of weapons research. In removing the obstacles separating human beings and communities, scientific and technological processes must be mobilized to deal with less selfish and dangerous concerns. The threats that technological development pose to humanity and its environment represent an alarm call to our consciousness of the need to consolidate a global society.

Only by stressing the importance of the human being in the context of the global society can we help to change the narrowness of vision among states and limit the phenomenon of the pursuit of short-term self-interest. Evolution towards a global society implies government action to encourage each society at national level to identify more closely with the 'society of the human community', to make that society a reality, and to identify with this higher level to the extent of placing strong and lasting limitations on the instincts of national selfishness. That is the challenge for those who govern.

In this enterprise, the first task at national level is for individuals and public institutions to give the best possible service, and to protect and promote human rights. Governments therefore need to give priority to strengthening the foundations of peace and human rights, to effective cultivation of responsible attitudes, and to the development of true democracy. These are essential conditions for growth and openness leading to better mobilization of resources, human and otherwise, in the service of the global society.

To achieve such a goal, the public sector must cultivate and maintain conditions ensuring that nationals from a given country no longer regard themselves as being in opposition to others, but as one expression of the rich diversity of human life. Thus it will provide a vibrant and dynamic framework in which individualities and particularities can acknowledge each other because all are expressing and supporting the consensus.

In their role as guardians and symbols of this consensus, therefore, governments inspired by the new ethic need to create conditions encouraging the acceptance of wider systems of values that go beyond the limited framework of the localized state. People will then begin to identify with foreign nationals and with the citizens of other countries, and any assertion of particularities at national or regional level will be complementary because the emphasis will be placed on human beings, and the essence of humanity is the same everywhere. States have already helped to bring about substantial scientific, technical and technological progress aimed at alleviating suffering and reducing the effects of disparities in resources. The way is open for the encounter of human beings at their highest level, and in this the public sector has a fundamental role to play as catalyst.

Adamou Ndam Njoya is a diplomat and a professor at the University of Cameroon. He has been a Counsellor and Vice-Minister in the Ministry of External Affairs and a Minister in the Department of Education in Cameroon, and has served on the Executive Assembly of UNESCO.

A NEW APPROACH TO THE WORLD PROBLEMATIQUE

Bertrand Schneider

The definition of 'world problematique' as it has been adopted at the first meeting of the Club of Rome is:

> The massive and untidy tangle of intertwining and interrelated difficulties and problems which form the predicament that mankind finds itself in.

The problematique will always be with humanity no matter how effective are the solutions we adopt. Changing situations, including those arising from the solution of existing problems, give rise to new difficulties. Furthermore, in times of rapid change, as at the present, the mix of problems and their relative importance is also likely to change rapidly. Thus, in the contemporary problematique the acuteness of the various elements is necessarily different from those outlined in the 'Limits of Growth' report of 1972, partly because our perceptions are clearer and more sophisticated, and partly because new knowledge has identified new dangers. Today the two most dominant elements are probably those of population increase and of the only recently recognized macroeffects on the environment caused by human activity.

Doom-saying is, of course, not our only role. It is merely a prelude to 'Doom-breaking'. The first report to the Club of Rome, 'The Limits of Growth', was not a prophecy but a warning of what might happen if policies were not changed in order to prove its forecasts wrong. Such a preventive approach carries with it the responsibility of putting forward suggested remedies.

I

The present situation

Let us note some of the main changes since 1972 and their consequences.

On the political side, there has been the diminishing dominance of the two superpowers with the fading out of ideological polarization and the ending of the cold war. Progress in disarmament is expected to continue, and the danger of nuclear annihilation has diminished so that the public feel less threatened, although nuclear war by accident remains possible and smaller rogue nations now possess the bomb. Lastly, there has been the collapse of communist dominance in Eastern Europe, with confused approaches to democracy and to economic restructuring.

On the economic side, there has been a movement of trade and manufacturing towards the Far East and the rise of the Newly Industrialized Countries (NICs). The period has seen the accumulation of massive debts, especially in Latin America, Africa and Eastern Europe but also dramatically in the United States, and the formation of three massive trade blocs: USA/Canada, the European Community, and the ASEAN countries and Japan. The situation of other countries vis-à-vis these trade blocs remains obscure. Military conflict within the blocs is less likely, but economic friction between them seems probable; and the role of the multinational corporations who operate within and between the blocs has yet to be ascertained. All in all, the period has seen a marked increase in the interdependence of nations, and a decrease in their sovereignty partly due to changing economic and political moves and partly caused by technological development.

The rise of nationalism, especially among small, newly emerging groups, will need to be accommodated within the new economic and political blocs, as will the flourishing of religious fundamentalism and the traditional concept of sovereignty which, through economic interdependence, bilateral and multilateral treaties, is gradually disappearing. Some countries remain highly dependent on others for raw materials and energy, while others need investments, technology transfer and training. This interdependence creates a new solidarity not yet fully accepted or understood. But the affirmation of individual cultural identities should be an important factor in enabling people and societies to overcome the feelings of powerlessness natural in the individual confronted with the global dimension.

Hopes for the rapid development of the poorer countries have not been fulfilled. Hunger, malnutrition, disease and poverty still afflict a large proportion of humanity and have been aggravated by population explosion, droughts and local wars. Increasing stocks of armament in the Third World countries, provided by the industrialized nations, not only represent a huge economic burden, but encourage military adventurism.

Application of peaceful new technologies, however, has progressed rapidly and has transformed world communications. There has been rapid development of information technology in the industrialized countries.

Automation has modified manufacturing processes and industrial structures, improving working conditions but also bringing unemployment; biological advances, while often questioned on ethical grounds, have yielded their first fruits in the improvement of plant and animal strains.

The period has also seen a growth in the general consciousness of threats to the environment, and the rise of the 'green movements'. Initially, attention was focused on essentially local pollution, phenomena that could be countered by local or national legislation and education, and considerable improvements have resulted. More recently, major environmental threats have been identified that are global in nature and cannot be tackled by individual countries in isolation. The most important of these macropollutions appears to be the 'greenhouse effect', which is an increase in the concentration of carbon dioxide in the atmosphere resulting from the combustion of fossil fuels and the extensive eradication of the tropical forests. This is expected to give rise to a substantial warming of the earth's surface and a rise in sea level. Great regions of the world, such as coastal areas of Bangladesh, and low-lying islands, are in danger of disappearing. It is doubtful if existing international mechanisms are capable of dealing with this new global phenomenon, which has many social and economic aspects.

Recent decades have also seen great changes in individual and social behaviour, and in the geopolitical situation. We have recently seen the rise of people's power, supported by a large part of world public opinion, which was crushed brutally in China, but has led to the downfall of the governments of the Eastern European countries, and is still evolving in Chile and in South Africa. Another dramatic factor has been the increase in fanaticism, exploding into violence and terrorism, as a result of social inequity and political oppression. In addition, the period has witnessed the sexual revolution, with the recognition of homosexuality. Related to this has been the appearance of the auto-immune disease AIDS, and major social problems resulting from the vastly increased extent of drug-taking. Some would wish to add to this sombre list an increase in individual, corporate, and national selfishness and corruption.

I want to focus now on some of these elements that deserve special attention. The concept of the world problematique indicates that all these issues are interconnected, and interactive, and it is difficult, therefore, to be specific as to how the situation is likely to evolve. We should start with the environmental threats, and examine their probable impact on other elements of the problematique. And this is directly linked to the behaviour of the private sector, and indeed of the public sector. The major macropollution phenomena recognized at present are acid rain, the accumulation of non-biodegradable toxins, the depletion of the ozone layer, and the greenhouse effect. While we shall concentrate on the greenhouse effect here, it must be remembered that these phenomena are themselves interactive. We must also note the fear that in a matter of decades, toxic materials in our soil and water may filter into the main aquifers.

What, then, are the main effects of the warming of the earth's surface and when are they likely to become acute? Present knowledge suggests that with present emission levels of carbon dioxide and other greenhouse gases, a warming of between 1.5 and 4.5 degrees centigrade will have taken place by about forty years hence. The warming will be negligible at the equator, and great at high latitudes, thus altering the thermal gradients of the planet, resulting in fundamental changes in patterns of precipitation and hence of soil fertility and food-producing capacity. It is not possible to forecast with any degree of certainty what the effect would be in any particular location, but it is suggested that some of the bread-basket areas such as the American Midwest and the Ukraine are likely to become much more arid. This could have a disruptive effect on world food security.

If the warming of the earth's surface is allowed to continue too long because of unrestrained emission of the greenhouse gases, it could become irreversible. There are, however, many measures that could be taken to slow it down and eventually to bring it to a halt; the fundamental need is to slow down the combustion of fossil fuels. The 1988 Toronto Conference of scientists suggested that if the situation were to be brought under control, it would be necessary to reduce the emission of carbon dioxide by twenty per cent by the year 2005. Thus the remedial measures themselves would have a damaging impact, unless alternative energy production can be available in time, because a reduction in energy levels could have a devastating effect on industrialization in the North and development in the South. This raises the awkward question as to whether environmental constraints will not merely limit growth, but actually reduce economic activity and necessitate a much more austere way of life in the industrialized countries. Can an economy based on stimulated consumption survive, or even expand enough to meet the development needs of the poorer countries, in the face of nature's constraints? These are key questions that demand discussion now. Politicians must not be allowed to evade them under the pretext of the uncertainty that persists about the exact extent of environmental constraints.

A second factor in the increasing concentration of carbon dioxide in the atmosphere is the disappearance of a large proportion of the earth's tropical forests, which previously absorbed quantities of the gas by photosynthesis in green leaves. Elimination of the forests is to be deprecated for many other reasons; it gives rise to local and regional climatic change, causes soil erosion and flooding downstream, and frequently leaves soils incapable of sustaining agriculture.

It is urgent, therefore, to bring a halt to the destruction of the forests and to introduce widespread programmes of afforestation, in view of the long period of growth necessary before their absorption capacity for carbon dioxide is fully developed. In the case of the poorer countries such efforts will need international financial support on a massive scale, but this can be justified by self-interest on the part of the donors, who have a vested interest in maintaining the global climate. It has to be appreciated that the afforestation problem is important also with regard to providing rural populations with fuel wood, which remains the main source of energy for a large proportion of mankind, and the lack of which is now generating great hardship.

II

Underdevelopment and population

We turn now to another element of the problematique, that of underdevelopment and population. Development remains a main priority, not only on humanitarian grounds, but because a continuing and growing disequilibrium between living standards of North and South as well as those of East and West would inevitably generate conflict. Present methods of attacking the problems of development are inadequate and in some cases counterproductive, and new approaches are essential.

The problems of the Third World are exacerbated by the population explosion. At the beginning of the century the world population was about 1.8 billion. It will have reached six billion by the year 2000 and is expected to level off at about ten to twelve billion by the middle of the next century. By far the greater part of this growth will have taken place in the less developed regions of the world. Indeed, in the industrialized nations demographic growth is very slow, and in some cases negative, leaving these nations with a whole series of new difficulties associated with aging populations.

Disparities of population will increase rapidly; by the middle of the century, inhabitants of the presently industrialized countries will constitute well under twenty per cent of the global population. It is impossible to envisage a future world in which a ghetto of rich nations arms itself with sophisticated weapons for protection against the hordes of hungry, uneducated, unemployed and angry people outside. More likely population pressures will have generated waves of mass emigration, impossible to contain, towards the North and the West. At the extreme it is possible to imagine innumerable immigrants landing from their boats on the Northern shores of the Mediterranean and forming an Islamic fringe in Southern Europe, consisting of the hungry and the desperate. Similarly, massive Latin American immigration into the United States is to be expected, while population pressure in China may overflow into empty Siberia. Such events would, of course, provoke opposition and one can envisage the rise of a series of right-wing dictators. And as we have already seen, the rise in sea level resulting from the greenhouse effect could greatly reinforce migration pressures.

Such situations must not be allowed to develop. Prevention lies in the improvement of economic conditions in the poor countries and in the introduction of effective methods of population control.

The breakdown of the economies of Eastern European countries and their movement towards democracy is naturally demanding a massive infusion of capital. The western countries, equally naturally, are responding, realizing the need for stability in Europe and hoping to find new markets. The dramatic nature of these events is tending to obscure the needs of the Third World countries which are, at least for the moment, losing the interest of donors.

III

Global food security

A few words must be said about the prospects for global food security. The success of agricultural production since the end of World War II has been phenomenal, and has led to a situation of considerable world surplus co-existing with vast areas of hunger and malnutrition, caused by drought and warfare. It is clear that the existence of abundant food in the world has little relevance to the persistence of hunger. The hungry are the poor, unable to buy food, so that hunger in large parts of the so-called Third World is but a symptom of the basic problem of poverty. The great food surpluses available for export exist in North America, on the success of whose harvests the deficit countries depend. Given the continuation of present patterns of agricultural production, the main deficit areas at the end of the century will be the Middle East, and also Africa, where a net annual deficit of sixty million tons is estimated.

But will the patterns persist? The droughts of 1988 sent a shock throughout the world food system. The drought in the United States appears to have been the most severe ever recorded, with grain production falling below domestic consumption. The US harvest fell by thirty-one per cent and that of Canada by twenty-seven per cent. The deficits were made good by the use of accumulated stocks, from which exports to the 100 countries that depend on food imports from North America were also maintained. The question arises as to what would happen if similar droughts were to occur frequently. It is not possible with any certainty to attribute the 1988 droughts to global warming, but the event was a clear warning of the vulnerability of food security to changes in climate.

Until about 1950, increases in agricultural production came mainly from the extension of land under cultivation. Thereafter, massive expansion was achieved through the use of chemical fertilizers. Agriculture no longer depends exclusively, therefore, on current solar energy, but is considerably dependent on fossil fuels – the stored solar energy of past aeons. It takes approximately a ton of oil to produce a ton of nitrogenous fertilizer. Petroleum is also required in the manufacture of pesticides and weed-killers as well as for tillage and irrigation pumps.

During the period 1950–86, the average world consumption of fertilizers per capita rose from 5 kg to 26 kg, while at the same time the area devoted to harvested cereals dropped from 0.24 to 0.15 hectares per capita. Thus, put crudely, the great increase in world food production represents the conversion of oil into edible cereals via the photosynthetic process. Future scarcity or high cost of oil, or restraints on usage forced by global warming, could greatly inhibit food production at a time when high population growth will demand more and more food.

A further danger point is the widespread degradation and erosion of the soil. Soil erosion is a natural process, but when its rate exceeds that of new soil formation, there is a decline in the productivity of the land. It is estimated that this is the situation in some thirty-five per cent of the world's crop-land. In regions of drought and overpopulation, land degrades quickly; in the North American bread-basket, topsoil is mined and unsuitable land cultivated to meet ever-growing demands for food from the world outside. Enormous amounts of topsoil with its nutrients are constantly washed away by the rains and rivers.

Intensive practices such as those of the 'green revolution' demand increased use of water. As a consequence, water levels are falling in many areas, throwing doubt on the sustainability of these practices. Greater use of irrigation has also increased water use in agriculture, causing salinization in many areas and destroying their agricultural potential. This, however, is only one element in the approaching crisis of global water availability. Increased domestic demand for water as well as industrial needs are growing rapidly, while the threat of its contamination by toxic wastes makes the availability and quality of water an increasingly sensitive area of the world problematique.

IV

Economic change

Great changes have also taken place on the economic front. After the period of rapid growth, recession set in simultaneously with the petroleum crisis and the recycling of the Arab surplus. During the past two decades the economic centre of gravity has moved emphatically towards the Pacific region, with the amazing success of the Japanese industrial economy. Japan, which now accounts for some thirty-eight per cent of the world's total financial capacity, has not yet learned how to exert its new-found strength; its political moves are cautious and tentative, and as yet it is internationally ineffective.

We are now witnessing the emergence of three gigantic trading and industrial blocs. The North American market in which Canada has now joined the United States, and which Mexico is to join later, will inevitably continue to be an industrial and post-industrial centre of great power. Its immediate future is, however, clouded by the immense deficit that it has allowed to accumulate in recent years.

The development of the European Community, despite the years of hesitation, is now acquiring substance as its members recognize the tangible economic and political advantage to be gained from co-operation and devise new mechanisms for it. As it achieves closer economic integration, the Community begins discussion of political unity. This is given special urgency with the unification of Germany. A Community embracing the whole of Western Europe, and later joined by their eastern neighbours when their economies make this possible, would constitute a second bloc of great strength. It is not impossible that the European republics of the former Soviet Union will one day follow the same road, eventually constituting de Gaulle's Europe from the Atlantic to the Urals.

The third bloc consists of Japan and the ASEAN countries – for example Thailand, Indonesia and Malaysia, which are growing rapidly. Later, perhaps Australia and New Zealand, which have strong trading links with the other Pacific countries, may find themselves in this grouping. Even at this early stage of development, the existence of these three blocs signifies an utterly different world pattern of trade and industry.

This prospect is of great concern to other regions of the world. Latin America, geographically close to the United States, but with a different ethos, is particularly perplexed; and while initiatives from its neighbour in the North are on the horizon, it is also reaching out towards Europe, with Spain perhaps acting as an intermediary. The republics of the former Soviet Union, in disarray, are not yet in a position to deal with this situation;

China, after the recent brutal events, remains an enigma; while poor Africa hardly appears on the world economic map.

Conflicts in a world dominated by huge trade blocs are likely to be very different from those of the world of nation-states. Wars between the constituent countries within a bloc would appear archaic, while wars between the blocs would more likely be economic than military. In this connection, the future role of the transnational corporations will probably become exceedingly important, since their interests and structures would permeate all these blocs.

The interdependence of nations

A further feature of the geopolitical scene is a belated recognition of the essentially global nature of many contemporary problems, which cannot be solved or even approached realistically by individual countries in isolation. This has long been the case in the economic field. One has only to remember how quickly the Wall Street crash in the 1930s spread to become a world depression, and how mass unemployment tends to appear simultaneously in many countries. This was no doubt an inevitable consequence of the great expansion of world trade in this century. More recently, global problems of a different nature have arisen. These range from environmental issues, through international legal questions such as the 'Law of the Sea' nego-tiations, to international finance. Recognition of this new situation, aware-ness of which came very slowly, is illustrated by the mushrooming of intergovernmental conferences and those of specialist professional and scien-tific organizations during the period under review. It is doubtful if present international structures are sufficiently effective to deal with them. The United Nations and its specialized agencies, founded in post-war euphoria, were designed to meet the needs of a world situation much simpler than that of today, and are increasingly inappropriate for present needs. The present de-idealized circumstances provide an opportunity as well as an imperative need for restructuring the United Nations system, reallocating the functions of the various agencies and programmes and providing a new focus. Present difficulties in revitalizing UNESCO show how difficult this will be.

Concern about the global environment has given rise to a number of ad hoc probings at different levels, including that of Heads of Government. As yet such attempts are avoiding the fundamental issues. It is to be hoped that common and universal action to combat global problems will greatly diminish inter-bloc conflict, for there has been a great increase in the interdependence of nations in this period. The rise of economic communi-ties, the need for a common approach to the global issues, the immense expansion of international communications and the activities of the transnational corporations are some of the contributing factors.

These, then, are some of the most pressing elements of the problematique. There are many others; for example, we have already issued two reports on microelectronics and society that discuss unemployment, the transformation of industry, the use of leisure, and influence on political systems and world communications. These matters are related to the preoccupations described above and also hint that developments in advanced technology could well increase still further the developmental disparities between the rich and the poor nations. Other areas of scientific advance, for example the new biology, are also relevant. Furthermore, we must give great emphasis to problems of education, which pervade the whole problematique.

The new problematique is generating new and hitherto unknown kinds of conflict. Economic conflict, environmental conflict and migrational conflict are already appearing on the world scene, and a new challenge has to be faced by the international community: will we be capable of identifying and preventing this new sort of war, or will the world be submerged in unprecedented disorder?

Individual responsibility, as well as societal responsibility, is becoming a major factor in progress, and I believe that in the 1990s this will be an unavoidable complement to the human rights issue, which has dominated the past decade.

The human being is the creator of the problematique and suffers its consequences. In recent years increases in affluence in the developed countries have not been accompanied by a corresponding sense of responsibility. The cultivation of a global responsibility both by the individual and by societies is one of the most urgent needs of the next decade. The human being is at the centre of the problematique, and therefore it demands a systematic approach, paying due attention to the instinctive and irrational elements inherent in human nature that make for an uncertain world.

V

The need for innovation in structure and policy

The description of the present situation as 'the Great Transition' is apt. The complex issues, sketched above, will lead inevitably to a world fundamentally different from that of the past and demanding new visions and new structures. The traditional institutions of society, invented for a world that no longer exists, do not have the adaptability necessary for finding and applying solutions to the new challenges. They are no longer in a position to govern effectively. All the pressing problems we have discussed need to be tackled simultaneously, within a holistic framework for which no mechanism exists. Faced with the complexity of the problems, the response of governments is often the creation of new agencies and still further growth of competitive bureaucracies which are often irresponsible, opposed to the global vision and incapable of looking beyond the short term.

The Club's unfinished work on 'Governability and the Capacity to Govern' is a recognition of the need for structural and institutional innovation. It is to be hoped that the 1990s will see the appearance of a whole range of new and imaginative structures, better adapted to the profound transformations that are rocking both national governments and world society. The reformed institutions of governments will be complemented by many and more effective NGOs, which should have greater influence on behalf of the individual citizen.

Recent years have indeed seen some advances for the freedom of the human spirit. The topic of human rights has even become politically fashionable. There is a world-wide trend for rigid and oppressive societies to collapse, as evidenced by events in Chile and Eastern Europe; it is to be hoped, however, that the peoples who are enthusiastically demanding democracy will not slavishly copy the existing models, which are fast becoming obsolete. The long-established democracies, which have functioned tolerably well during the past 200 years, seem to have grown old and, in their complacent stagnation, show little evidence of real leadership and innovation. The new age demands new visions, new policies, new structures and new people.

Search for a new system of ethical values

The double standards of adults *vis-à-vis* young people or political leaders *vis-à-vis* ordinary citizens create a credibility gap, cast doubt on the validity of their assertions and illustrate the major contradictions disrupting our societies. They disturb the young, who no longer know who or what to believe. How, then, in this vacuum, are we to avoid bewilderment or the temptation of various forms of nihilism, fundamentalism or ultra-conservatism? The quest for a vision of a new world inspired by a global solidarity and fraternity seems still without proper answers from the traditional centres of wisdom such as churches, religious communities, spiritual leaders and philosophers.

In societies threatened by break-up, human beings, rootless and pulled in all directions, are searching for common values and compatible visions of the future. Amid the weariness of the world they feel a vital need to rebuild – but sometimes to destroy – to bring people together again and to free themselves from the thousand absurdities that obstruct their search for unity, purpose and self-fulfilment. In short, they feel the need to pave the way for a rebirth of humanity compatible with the reality of their new environment.

This rebirth cannot take place immediately or without pain. It cannot disregard the diversities of societies and cultures, discount the burden of tradition or forget that words and concepts do not always have the same meaning in different languages. Such a quest must not yield to the temptation of seeking unanimity by ignoring disagreements, or admit defeat at the first signs of the perils of such an ambitious and difficult undertaking.

Educational systems

The permanent quest of humanity for new values to permit an equitable and harmonious way of life for both societies and individuals is an essential part of the global problematique. And this quest is a challenge to all educators and the systems of education as a whole, combining the complementary and converging impact of family, school and media. We must return to the ancient concept that life and education form a 'continuum' from birth until death. This explains why education and its necessary reshaping is part of the problematique and a tool for understanding a rapidly changing world and for learning to adapt to change.

In short, we need a fundamental reappraisal of the education system aimed much more at values than curricula. This reappraisal must be taken to its logical conclusion, which is the abolition of all barriers, the development of a two-way learning process through communicative exchanges of know-how, with self-educated persons continually improving their knowledge, and priority given to interdisciplinarity through teamwork.

Increasing disparities between human beings who have access to education and knowledge and those who, for cultural or personal reasons, have not, might lead to the marginalization of great numbers of people in the developing countries. In the developed world also, disparity between those who know and those who do not know leads to a society with two classes of citizenship, encourages technocracy and leads to alienation. The creation of two categories of citizens functioning at two different levels would be a very serious destabilizing factor, and must be avoided in the education systems of the future.

Bertrand Schneider is the Chairman of SYCOR, an international communications group, and the Secretary-General of the Club of Rome. He has been the Secretary-General of the National Committee for Medical Care (France) since 1968.

ONE WORLD – ONE VISION FOR WORLD BUSINESS

Dieter Tober

I

Globalization: A megatrend in politics and economics

We are all aware of the concept of the 'One World' without physical or mental barriers, as reflected in the satellite pictures of 'Mother Earth' showing a colourful and bright planet, perfectly round, harmonious and peaceful in a dark universe. Everyone knows, too, that our real world is quite different, and that the One World concept is a dream. Dream it may be, but it is one that is gradually being realized in both political and economic spheres. In line with the general trend of globalization, the goal of One World appears to be gaining more and more support and is becoming more and more clearly defined. Global thinking is clearly gaining momentum, and covers a broad spectrum of issues and scenarios. How and why did it come about? I shall focus on just a few of the many origins of the globalization process.

Firstly, we must consider the effects of liberalization by deregulation and denationalization. It all started in the United States with the liberalization of air traffic and heavy goods transport under Jimmy Carter. A major step forward occurred when Margaret Thatcher came to power in the United Kingdom. This was closely followed by the beginning of the Reagan administration in 1980, the change of government in Germany in 1982, and the shift in France's economic policy after 1981–2. Many countries began to adopt free-market and deregulation policies, often accompanied by denationalization of state-owned industries.

Secondly, there is the role of modern technology, in particular telecommunications and information. Satellites are capable of storing and transmitting vast amounts of data, pictures and information. Three satellites in a carefully planned geostationary position enable all human beings to communicate with each other across continents and time-zones. Television, telephone, fax and other electronic media add to this barrier-free exchange of information. Databanks expand with phenomenal speed, and can be used world-wide in direct communication. According to recent estimates, in the business sector alone more than two thousand databanks are currently operating around the globe. Major qualitative and quantitative improvements in transport and logistics have similarly helped humanity to overcome the limitations of space and time; the distinguished historian Arnold Toynbee described our age as one characterized by the 'destruction of distance'. Technological innovations have indeed enabled millions of people to widen their horizons, making our world both bigger and more accessible for the individual.

Thirdly, there are pressing global issues such as population growth, pollution of the air, soil and water, global warming, the depletion of the ozone-layer, over-consumption of natural resources, issues about energy use, waste disposal, and achieving sustainable development. This sample of the many key issues clearly shows the need for a 'greening' of politics, economics and our general social behaviour.

II

Configurations of world business

The heavyweights in world business are the US, Japan and Germany, known to economists as the 'Triad'. In 1988 they generated, between them, around forty per cent of world gross product and almost one third of world exports. For the entire globe, economists use the model of the 'Hexagon', consisting of the US, Japan, the European Community, the former COMECON countries, newly industrialized countries (NICs) and less developed countries (LDCs). These are the principal configurations of world business.

Let us look at some important problem areas in trade relations between major groups of countries.

The *North–South Problem* describes the delicate relationship between rich and poor, or developed and developing countries. Some basic figures show the extent of the problems:

- Industrial countries account for two thirds of world trade (1985); given the centuries-old traditions of these trading nations, this is no surprise.
- While almost four fifths of North–South exports are industrial goods, two thirds of South–North exports are raw materials and agricultural products.
- The proportion of raw materials (excluding oil) and foodstuffs in world trade is slowly diminishing.
- Progress in industrialization by a few developing countries is creating

new markets for the products of developing countries. At the same time, however, the traditional trading nations are being ousted from markets for some industrial goods in these countries. Although many industrial nations grant trading concessions to the developing countries, these concessions are often counteracted by restrictions on market access. Furthermore, industrial nations produce high agricultural surpluses and still largely subsidize their agro-industries from public funds, thereby building new barriers to market access and dumping the surpluses on the markets at the taxpayer's expense.

The *North–North Problem* is one of trade relations between the industrial countries. They have long developed a very high degree of 'international division of labour', necessarily leading to international interdependence. An upswing in economic activity in one country has the effect of boosting demand in countries experiencing a downswing. In the early 1980s, for example, the United States acted as an 'economic locomotive' in this way for Japan and Western Europe. More recently, the EC countries reciprocated towards the US economy.

The *West–East Problem* was for many decades dominated by economic stagnation in Eastern Europe. The per capita national product of the 423 million inhabitants of the European division of COMECON was $5700 in 1988, while that of western industrial nations was over two and a half times that amount, namely $14,800. For Eastern Europe to match the western level of prosperity, its per capita national product would have to increase by ten per cent annually over a period of ten years.

Eastern Europe is also under-represented in world trade. Although 8.2% of the world's population lives in the European countries of COMECON, they supply only seven per cent of international exports. By contrast the European Community, representing approximately six per cent of the world population, accounts for thirty-seven per cent of international exports.

In the past, an important trade barrier was the list drawn up by the Co-ordinating Committee for East–West Trade (COCOM). In the process of unification, Germany is striving hard to streamline this list, in order to afford easier access to western technology.

The *East–South Problem* arose with the political and economic opening-up of Middle and Eastern Europe and the introduction of free-market systems in the former COMECON countries. In particular the LDCs fear they will be crowded out by an enforced diversion of international capital to the reforming economies of Eastern Europe. With a debt mountain of

roughly $1200 billion according to IMF figures, they indeed depend on
further capital influx, this having decreased from $51 billion net in 1981 to
a meagre $1.3 billion in 1989. Meanwhile billions in hard currency were set
aside for the establishment of the European Bank of Reconstruction and
Development, and despite huge debts ($41 billion and $21 billion respectively), more than eleven billion ECU were assigned to Poland and Hungary.

The immense capital needs of Eastern Europe will clearly be detrimental
to the LDCs. A solution to this problem could lie in an international
division of labour, with Western Europe leading the help for Eastern
Europe, and the US and Japan taking responsibility for their own regions.
Finance for Africa would have to be provided by all public creditors.

Inter-Group Trade, that is trade between the developing countries, and
particularly between industrial nations, is on the increase. Two main causes
can be identified:

- A specific form of international division of labour is prevalent. There
  is a growth of trade in products manufactured in rival trading nations
  to a similar level of sophistication using similar production techniques.
  For many industrial goods, the main customers are also the chief suppliers.
- Consumer living conditions and demand patterns are similar in countries enjoying comparable levels of development. Similar costs and production structures narrow the gulf between competitors.

Inter-industrial trade will undoubtedly be beneficial for future world trade.
The international division of labour will open up low cost-structures, all
countries involved can profit, and rival trading nations will not deprive one
another of export opportunities. Even the export successes of NICs, which
will help to create additional trade in some industrial sectors, need not harm
the traditional industrial countries.

III

Prevailing trends towards a multipolar world

Economists see a continual progressive trend towards further international-
ism among the economies of the world, reflected in mounting national
export and import quotas and the growing importance of cross-border
mergers and acquisitions. Simultaneously they see an increase in regional
integration of economies, a convergence of seemingly contradictory trends
which has been described as 'globalization with increased regionalization'.

This is exemplified by East Asia, where successful export-oriented economic growth has been accompanied by rapid structural change. Between 1978 and 1988, Hong Kong, Singapore, South Korea and Taiwan had an average annual growth rate of more than seven per cent: some four per cent higher than that enjoyed by OECD countries.

Bilateralism, in some cases combined with compensation trade, accounts for part of the regionalization trend. For example, the Free Trade Agreement between the United States and Canada, which became effective early in 1989, created the biggest bilateral trade bloc in the world. The European Single Market, soon to become the largest of its kind in the free world, will be characterized by many special bilateral trade relations, for example between France and Germany, or the UK and the Netherlands. Bilateral 'voluntary restraint agreements' between individual EC nations and third countries are intended to restrict the importation of specific goods, such as cars. It has also been agreed that, from 1994 onwards, there will be closer co-operation between the European Single Market and the EFTA countries.

The EC holds great attraction for the remaining EFTA countries, for neutral countries like Austria, and for the new free market economies of Poland and Hungary, anxious to become members as quickly as possible. Even in Switzerland, discussion has begun as to whether a neutral status can be sustained next to such a powerful market.

Regionalization is visible at local, regional, national and international levels. There is strong competition between business areas at all levels. Local, provincial, federal or central state authorities are being pressured by their respective industries into creating favourable investment conditions. In this context a suitable legal and fiscal framework is needed, along with improvements in infrastructure, logistics and telecommunications, and a skilled work-force, all combining to create a positive business climate conducive to entrepreneurial action.

The One World, from this perspective, will for many years to come be a multipolar world with many economic centres and considerable disparities in public and private wealth between geographic areas and even within the various areas. While East Asia, Western Europe and North America prosper, Africa and Latin America are likely to face big problems with their enormous foreign debt burden, and will lag behind.

Are we facing a world of two or more speeds in growth and development? We have to ensure that increased regionalization does not bring about global disintegration. For example, the more third country exports to the EC are replaced by regional internal trade, the more outsiders will lose access to markets. One of the foremost tasks of GATT will be to liberalize markets whenever and wherever possible. A 'fortress Europe' or 'Japan Inc.' would be detrimental to free world trade and integration into world markets. According to the late Alfred Herrhausen, who was Chief Executive of the Deutsche Bank and one of the most innovative figures in international finance, 'the name "developing countries" describes a geopolitical programme; these countries will develop themselves. If they do so, even the developed countries will benefit within the context of the one world in which we live.'

An increase in North–South conflicts would obviously strengthen polarization instead of integration, leading inevitably to huge waves of migration. In addition to economic pressure, this would fuel conflicts between national, ethnic, religious or social minorities.

IV

Limits to world economic integration: protectionism

Among the major obstacles to world economic integration is protectionism, that is, foreign trade policies which are designed to protect domestic manufacturers against foreign competition. Among the instruments used in the pursuit of protectionism are customs duties and administrative and other trade barriers.

Since I come from Germany, a country highly dependent on free world trade, you may accept my proposition that fair competition requires equal opportunities. Distortions in competition still prevail, however. Market prices have to compete with government-controlled prices. Developing countries expect preferential terms. Industrial nations are becoming increasingly vulnerable and sensitive to the artificial competitive advantages enjoyed by the NICs. Furthermore, services are playing an increasingly substantial part in the international division of labour. For example, in the United States and the United Kingdom, exports of services have reached the same level as exports of goods. Services include the international supply of patents, licences and data as well as the provision of consultancy and engineering services to other countries. The sector also encompasses the transport, insurance and financial services that accompany trade in capital goods and plant construction, and are now almost as important as the product itself.

Up to now the GATT rules have not applied to services, making competition in the services sector vulnerable to distortion. New solutions need to be elaborated within GATT to strengthen liberalism and avert the danger of a global trade war.

V

The corporate business world
Business, in particular big business, plays a leading role in the process of globalization. The various categories are generally labelled 'global players', 'world-class players', 'major players', and 'niche players': respectively, corporations with a world-wide network of production and distribution facilities; corporations with comparatively little exposure in international business, but with a world-class or partly world-class format; and specialists in product, service or regional niches. These classifications are used for industrial, banking, insurance and other service conglomerates.

The key parameters of a 'global player' are: size by turnover, capital, work-force, market share, position within the industry sector, world-wide on-the-spot presence, interrelation of production and distribution centres, production and innovation potential, capital spread, and mixed management. 'We are locals world-wide', as Ervin Laszlo remarked the other day, quoting an advertisement.

What is the key role of these multinational companies? For decades they have contributed heavily to economic growth, development and industrialization of developing countries by direct investment. Most LDC governments are striving for export growth to bring them valuable foreign exchange earnings, as well as for reduced dependence on imports. The majority of multinationals contribute prominently to the capital and service balance and generate additional direct and indirect taxes. The surplus is increased by tax payments on local supplies of goods and services to these multinationals. They create job opportunities, offer higher income and better working conditions, with positive effects on local companies.

Is further internationalization politically acceptable? Up to now, trade unions and workers in the West have sharply criticized companies wishing to move to other countries. Yet further restructuring of western industries is inevitable. We are part of the world economy, and our solidarity can no longer be confined to a national level, but must take on a global perspective, even if this brings disadvantages in some cases. This may well be the only chance for those countries and regions of whose economic plight we complain so much. Open borders and international engagement are necessary components of a global economic order supporting international equilibrium and reducing disparities and distortions. Only thus will the North–South problems I have outlined be solved.

The international division of labour will continue to generate more and more specialization, depending on climatic and geological factors, special skills, know-how, and basic economic conditions such as the availability of a skilled work-force, cheap capital, and efficiency of infrastructure, transportation, communication and information.

Global banking – global finance

The vision of One World appears to be highly advanced in the fields of banking and finance. In particular, foreign exchange markets must be the most sophisticated global market in existence. Throughout the world, foreign exchange transactions equivalent to more than $700 billion are carried out daily. In London alone, the main centre for foreign exchange dealings, the daily turnover is estimated at some $190 billion. In New York, another major centre, the volume is almost seven times what it was in 1980. Less than five per cent of these transactions are said to be directly connected with 'real' foreign trade. Similar findings are reported from international markets in credit, money, capital, stocks and commodities. The universal acceptance of financial innovations also reflects the globalization of banking and finance.

VI

The different stages of internationalization

The different stages in internationalization are best analysed by taking the case of my own country, the Federal Republic of Germany, as an example.

- *Trade expansion*: German enterprise accepted the challenge of internationalization after World War II. Starting from a relatively small home market, trade with western neighbours was extended. In 1968, the export and import quota of our economy was around twenty per cent. Today it has reached more than thirty per cent on average. Some major industry sectors even exceed fifty per cent, for example vehicle production, electronics, heavy machinery and chemical industries.
- Following the internetting of trade, *foreign investments* increased from DM 2 billion in 1968 to almost DM 20 billion in 1988.
- Meanwhile the third stage of going international, *overall internationalization*, has been reached. Corporations no longer limit their activities to purchase and marketing, but embrace all business activities: production, research and development, personnel and finance. Even co-operation with foreign partners, from licensing to joint ventures, is included, as is the whole business policy of German multinational companies.

Reasons for this new dimension of internationalization include:

- Innovation competition: life cycles of products get shorter, research and development has to be reinforced, investments in modern equipment increase. The costs can only be recouped in the bigger markets in Europe and the whole world.
- Customers demand local suppliers. In many cases the most sophisticated products are developed or adapted in close co-operation with the customer.
- Small national regions integrate to form larger, supranational business areas, for example the European Single Market, the North American and South American Free Trade Zones.
- Physical presence needs strengthening in areas with the highest growth rates, such as South-East Asia. Simply exporting is no longer sufficient.
- The banking industry has to take into account imbalances in international trade, deficits in the balances of payments, foreign exchange rates or the level of foreign indebtedness in the various partner countries.

VII

Reinforcing the institutional framework

What can be done to reinforce the One World approach in world business?

Extended responsibilities should be given to supranational organizations such as the World Bank, the IMF and GATT. Having a well-established track record in dealing with problems and issues of a global dimension, these institutions can meet the challenges of the hour in an increasingly complicated world only when restructured and empowered by capital and support, both public and private. National governments should not be reluctant to give their backing, even if it means transferring some economic sovereignty to these supranational bodies.

In addition, some in-depth study of the Canadian proposal for a World Trade Association merits consideration. This could perhaps integrate with GATT, and develop increased co-operation and fine-tuning with the World Bank and IMF.

Interrelation in world business

In the context of dealing with global problems such as the foreign debt crisis, protection of the environment or disarmament, the following adage has often been quoted: 'We should think globally but act locally.' This perfectly matches the needs of the One World.

Of course, there cannot be only *one* vision for One World in business. What is more important is to become conscious of the interrelation and interdependence of all problems, to develop common strategies and to engage in step-by-step activities: in short, to create *a* vision of One World, a joint endeavour of North and South, East and West. It is ideas that inspire and enrich mankind. One World, one business world.

Dieter Tober is Assistant General Manager at Georg Hauck & Sohn Bankiers KGaA, a German private bank based in Frankfurt. He is active in the field of corporate finance and a regular speaker at both national and international conferences.

PART 3

THE ROLE OF TECHNOLOGY
AND CULTURE
IN THE TRANSITION

THE PLACE OF INFORMATION TECHNOLOGY IN GLOBAL CHANGE

Ian O. Angell

I

We are all acutely aware of the phenomenal global changes, both societal and organizational, happening all around us. It is accepted wisdom that we are entering the sophistication of an *Information Age*,[1] led by the telecommunications revolution. Everywhere, the convergence of computer and communication technologies is seen as highly beneficial, and as an agent of change that will facilitate the transition to a global society. Governments and organizations all over the world have rushed headlong into what can only be called a technology binge, in the confident belief that lavish spending on information technology (IT) will ensure success and progress, and a future among the 'information rich'.

If only it was that simple! For we would be deceiving ourselves if we saw the slightest comfort in the title of this paper. I believe that, far from easing the transition to a global society, information technology is actually going to make things more complicated. I will justify this assertion with a number of detailed observations, starting with the statement that there is no way to comprehend the full implications of IT; prediction of its emergent behaviour is nigh on impossible. Information Technology is itself in transition, although transition may be too subdued a word to describe its volatility. We have a mistaken faith in its benefits and in its ability to solve problems. I will stress the importance of attempting to understand its behaviour, at least in hindsight, and I will use a simple analogy to clarify my explanation. From this position I will indicate how misunderstandings can arise, which in turn introduce surprising side-effects on human and organizational behaviour, making control impossible. This will lead to a recognition of the international ramifications, and I will end with the contention that a new sophistication is needed among IT professionals, their governments, employers and educators, if IT is to ease the global transition, and not make things far worse by adding layer upon layer of confusion.

II

A capricious technology?

Granted there are countless benefits from information technology, but these advantages do not come to us for free. We may think we know the price of IT, but there is no way to calculate total costs, because we do not comprehend the nature of the beast. The price may be levied here and now, but the cost accumulates from here to eternity. So most evaluation deals with long-term commitment on the basis of short-term factors such as efficiency and effectiveness. In line with other technologies (such as coal-mining or nuclear) the long-term costs of the inevitable phasing-out of old systems are not included in the calculations. Rarely is obsolescence allowed for, nor is there any recognition that non-productivity at the obsolescence stage can be destabilizing to an organization. Indeed Joseph Weizenbaum[2] goes as far as to say that the information technology is itself a missed opportunity to replace outdated organizational and societal structures. It prevents competitive progress by prolonging these obsolete structures behind a protective façade of computerized efficiency. When the crash comes, as it must, the damage will be substantially worse.

There is a real confusion about the characteristics of what is, after all, a very complex and uncertain challenge. This challenge we face with a singular lack of understanding. Information technology is itself in transition on a global scale, and we have no clear grasp as to what it really is, where it is going, or whether it is even a single convergent technology. The seemingly innocuous statement I made earlier, about the convergence of computer and communication technology, could in fact be a falsehood. This assertion gives the impression that both technologies are of equal status. Perhaps it is communication, and not calculation, that is driving change and giving the apparent commercial advantage. Perhaps computers are mere support for communication. Maybe computers are just a solution looking for a problem; a solution with doubtful merits. Perhaps what we have is a number of different technologies, and their vague classification under one label is going to cause even more confusion.

We just do not know the implications of applying the tools of this technology in societal and organizational arenas, because it is only with hindsight that we can recognize the phenomena that emerge when it is placed in those environments. The screens in a City of London investment house began blanking out every ten seconds, and telephone conversations were scrambled. They were worried about industrial espionage or malicious computer hackers. The trouble was actually caused by the radar system of H.M.S. *Coventry*, which was at anchor outside on the River Thames

(*Sunday Times*, 11 February 1990). Such peculiarities can easily be avoided, but there are more permanent and all-pervasive emergent phenomena, such as unsolicited or junk mail. Without computerized mailing lists and word-processing, junk mail would not be cost effective. Automating the mailing process reduces the cost to the sender, but at the price of inconvenience and annoyance to the receiver. Adding yet more sophistication makes it even easier for the sender, but correspondingly more expensive for the receiver: low fax charges now make the cost of junk-fax negligible compared with an average total of a little less than £1 per letter by conventional mail, and it has the added advantage of targeting higher socio-economic groups. Apart from the problem that junk can delay the receipt of important faxes, to add insult to injury, the receiver even has to pay for the paper on which the message is printed (4p a sheet). It is not surprising that suppliers of fax-paper were among the first to recognize the opportunities of junk-fax! Similarly, computer viruses can be viewed as an emergent phenomenon. Of course, by analogy with biological systems it was only to be expected that certain forms of parasites and diseases would emerge as computer systems became more complex. However, their specific forms could not be predicted and were only apparent in hindsight.

The universal problem-solver?

So why is information technology self-perpetuating? Why is it so success-ful? Is it because it is being sold like the cure-alls of the old 'patent medicine shows'? Of course technological panaceas are nothing new. In its pioneering days, electricity was claimed to have a therapeutic effect on the physiological processes of the body. Small electric shocks were thought to cure, among other things, consumption, dysentery, cancer, blindness and worms. The history of human problem-solving is littered with examples of the first-step fallacy:[3] they think they are reaching for the moon, but all they've done is climbed the nearest tree. It is very rare that the initial specific success of a particular approach can be generalized. This fact is highlighted by another example from medicine: after the success of anti-toxins in combating diphtheria and tetanus, the feeling among many medical companies was that:

> 'all disease would soon be conquered by anti-toxins'. It seemed so easy. All that needed to be done was to grow the germs in quanti-ties, filter off the toxin, inject it into horses in increasing quantities until the anti-toxin was good and strong, draw off some of the horse's blood, let it clot, inject the serum into a human patient and he was safe.[4]

This simple procedure was tried for almost every known disease. And so it is with high-profile IT procedures. Early success and enthusiasm, with for example artificial intelligence and decision-support systems, soon degenerate into rejection because of their failure to satisfy the hype of unrealistic and unjustifiable expectations. Then sensible applications are lumped together with the nonsense, and potentially beneficial projects fail to get support. Russell Ackoff describes this most forcibly in 'Management misinformation systems'.[5] But all is not gloom. It is instructive to look at where information technology has been successful; arguably, it is in solving well-structured and well-understood problems, problems that could be solved previously, but can now be worked out much faster by machine. These are solutions that previously involved hum-drum repetition, or that could be enhanced by rapid communication. However, in all these cases the advantage is not intrinsic to the technology, but to the capacity of resourceful people to use it.

Hidden agenda behind the benevolent technology?

So what is the harm in IT? The ritual application of information technology is reducing the anxiety of so many businessmen and politicians facing the profound uncertainty of our rapidly changing world. But it is lulling them into a misguided confidence in its own virtues. This again is nothing new; most developing technologies are seen as benevolent, that is until their full implications are understood. It is only after the nonsense stops that a technology can be used to its full potential. In the early days, X-rays were considered a harmless novelty, used unguarded to check on foot size in shoe shops, and to make a photographic souvenir for newlyweds, bride and groom clasping skeletal hands showing brand new wedding rings. Computers too can damage your health. There are numerous reports of repetitive strain injury, and recently three computer workers from the UK Inland Revenue were awarded a total of £107,500 damages, because they each developed 'tennis elbow' while keypunching data (*Daily Express*, 13 March 1990).

But there are pandemic disorders too. Far too often, information technology is considered culturally neutral, when in reality it is value-laden, and hides a powerful intellectual imperialism. This predicament is nothing new; it is the culmination of a trend that was recognized nearly two hundred years ago by Edmund Burke, the English politician, when he said: 'The Age of Chivalry is gone. That of economists, sophisters and calculators has succeeded; and the glory of Europe is extinguished for ever.' For behind much application of information technology is the malignant belief that human thought is mere calculation. There is a sinister hidden agenda stemming from the dominance of two ideas: that a number can be a meaningful representation of human experience; and that arithmetical operations on such representations, implemented on a computer, can produce 'rational decisions' about the human condition. Computer simulations maintain a pretence that they represent reality within their limited models, but they really cannot hope to emulate the infinity of parameters implicit in 'being there'. The application of IT obscures the difference between correlation and causality, and confuses superficial process with substance. The values of accountancy, in so-called 'Information Audits' and 'Expert Systems', imply that all decisions can be reduced to a form of algorithmic book-keeping. Performance measures are manipulated by computer programmes in a ritualistic fashion, more akin to 'reading the runes' than to any legitimate science. The futurologists and gurus of IT are just another example of the blind leading the blind, in a frenzied dance of sophistry, economics and calculation.

Everywhere there is the quest for efficiency, where any form of redundancy in the data is viewed as inefficiency that must be eliminated. This perverse and decadent view of efficiency was anticipated by Northcote Parkinson,[6] when he warned that 'perfection in planning is a symptom of decay'. For redundancy is not waste. It has its uses. It can help reinforce or reject values, allow for human forgetfulness and for social checks and balances, allow for error tolerance, and give time to reflect and reconsider. Unfortunately the prevalent distortion of 'scientific management' portrays all of these as human faults, to be corrected in the world of the virtuous machine. But this brave new world will not be one of ordered, constrained and controlled lives; it will be a rule-based bureaucratic shambles.

III

The analogy of the 100% guaranteed 'universal roach exterminator'
Information technology has permeated the whole international business infrastructure, and IT is now essential for commercial survival. Modern management must come to grips with IT, for it has gone far beyond the claims of competitive advantage. But examples of the 'big killing' advanced in the IT literature are almost certainly lucky accidents of being in the right place at the right time. Such individual cases can be no basis for future planning. Planning must be left in the hands of 'thinking managers', whose experience is learned the hard way and is based on intuition and on a solid intellectual base. What is not needed is a breed of management automaton, weaned on a simplistic technological creed.

Managers have to develop a variety of approaches in order to cope with the impact of IT. But to do this, some comprehension of its behaviour is necessary. In my teaching I have found it very useful to use an analogy[7] that goes some way towards illuminating the situation. The analogy is a metaphor for my own personal reasons for retreating from the arrogance of technocratic certainty. However, it is not meant as a denial of information technology, but only as a recognition of its limitations.

The analogy is with the universal roach exterminator, sold by mail-order in the US to solve the problem of cockroach infestation. It consists of hardware (a mallet and a block of wood) and software (the list of operating instructions, 1: catch the cockroach; 2: place it on the block; 3: hit it with the mallet). Step 3 is relatively straightforward, but of course it does depend to a certain extent on step 2. For if the operator is too slow the cockroach will escape, too fast and he will hammer his thumb. So operational guidelines must be assembled; and naturally the equipment has to be purchased, stored, maintained and transported; carcasses must be removed; hygiene procedures must be developed. No doubt further tools will be produced to deal with each of these new situations. But it doesn't end there. The use of the tool may have unforeseen consequences: perhaps your pet piranha has a taste for cockroaches; neighbours may complain about the noise; animal-rights activists may demonstrate; one of the cockroaches could have been Archy, Mehitabel's biographer, and the world would have lost a great poet, philosopher and 'systems thinker';[8] you may even wake up screaming with nightmares about giant cockroaches. As with the case of every other technology, before we know it, the implications are running out of control, and a highly complex system has exploded onto the scene. Welcome to the real world, one of phenomena, not functionality.

Of course, this particular 'mallet technology' is ridiculous, because nothing has been gained by its application. All along the real solution was not killing a cockroach but catching it in the first place, a reality quietly hidden away in the first step of the software. But no doubt some 'trap technology' can be developed to overcome this, so that step 2 can begin. Laughable as this example may be, it does have parallels with technology in general, and with information technology in particular, and it does teach some salutary lessons. Before all else, a problem has to be sensed, and solutions/actions situated (step 1). Then a great deal of 'housekeeping' must be done (step 2), before we can apply the tools of the technology (step 3). But the analogy also shows that a technological solution is not applied in a vacuum. It has to be properly managed so as to achieve its intended aims, while at the same time dealing with any implications of its use, avoiding any emergent risks while profiting from any unexpected opportunities that may arise (step 2). But these risks and opportunities must be sensed as problems and solved (step 1), and the positive feedback loop is closed.

Dealing with technology in these abstract terms, we can see that what is commonly referred to as information technology actually only relates to the production and application of tools and artefacts (step 3). Managing both the technology and the complex systems that spontaneously manifest themselves around information technology is the domain of information systems (step 2). However, prevailing over them both is the dominant requirement of intelligent human response, to sense a problem and to identify what is appropriate and inappropriate action (step 1). So my warning to anyone too confident about developing a management information system is 'think cockroaches'.

In a 'scientific society' such as ours, the dominant paradigm is to formulate every new solution in terms of technology, even to sense the situation as being a problem specifically because of the potential of that technology: 'give a boy a hammer, and he will look for nails' (although our example has introduced a technology-inspired paradigm shift, so that now the boy will also look for cockroaches). Our predominant 'information ideology',[9] of aiming yet more information technology at any or all of our three steps, will only expand each step into a further three corresponding steps. This will introduce more complexity to an already complicated situation. Thus, arguably, the most successful applications of information technology have been:

1   where there is a real need, and the sensing of the problem and the situating of the solution (step 1) are reasonably straightforward (there have probably been well-structured manual systems previously in place), and

2   where the technology is reasonably stable, and not too complex to manage (because of the above, and because the inevitable extra effort is more than compensated for by savings in managing the old manual system), and

3   where the technology itself (step 3) is non-problematical and appropriate, and

4   where the consequences of applying the tools are limited, and the feedback loop is broken so that no further management problems are introduced.

However, initial success with IT can induce managers to introduce more and yet more layers of technology. To justify the extra effort and expense, managers will look around for partners in search of that mystical pot of

gold, 'synergy', that they read about in management books. The implications of using each new layer of technology will feed back in the form of
new questions about the appropriateness of solutions, and new management
problems. The original clear demarcation of three steps collapses in a confusion of multiplicity. Complexity increases to a point where utility turns
into reliance, reliance becomes dependence, and the law of diminishing
returns precipitates a descent into a management nightmare. Ultimately,
within this feedback loop, the self-serving logic will take on a significance
far greater than the original problem. Both the sensing of problems and the
situating and managing of solutions becomes impossible, and the whole
edifice of this 'information ideology' falls apart.

It is evident that an expectation of long-term utility from information
technology, given the global changes we are facing, is going to require a
whole new approach to the subject. Even if we stress the dominance of
communication over computerization, the problem remains. It is self-
evident that it is not the channel of communication that is significant (step
3), but the information that is being transmitted and the reasons for its
transmission (step 1), and how it is being used (step 2).[10] To date, computer
education and business applications have concentrated on the last of the
three steps in our 'information domain', when it is apparent that the seeds
of both success and failure germinate in the first two steps. Information
technology should be written with a capital 'I' and a small 't', for without
human input information becomes mere data, and has no intrinsic value.
And it does beg the question of whether we really are dealing with communication, or merely connection. To justify this opinion, I will now use
the three-step perspective to discuss some of the complexities that have
emerged from the application of IT. And I will demonstrate that it is only
with hindsight that we can both observe their effect and deal with the
problems that they cause for understanding and managing the technology.

IV

Human dimension and computer dimension

Computers can deal with objective well-structured problems with amazing
speed, but they cannot cope with subjective subtlety and ambiguity. There
is a basic management problem with integrating computerized information
systems with human activity systems, because they are fundamentally different. Computers do not work in physical space but in a mathematical dimension, a subtle fact too easily forgotten until it is too late. In August 1987
there was a collision between two RAF Tornado fighters on separate low-
flying night exercises over Cumbria. Based at different airfields, the planes

were using the same programme on their onboard computers. A cassette, given to each navigator before take-off, flies the plane automatically to avoid obstacles like hills and electricity pylons. Although coming from different directions, the planes arrived at exactly the same spot simultaneously, hence the crash (*Sunday Times*, 11 March 1990). What no one had realized was that the computer programme had reduced the flying space of three dimensions into a single linear path, where the planes could not avoid one another. This oversight has now been corrected.

The checks and balances fundamental to error tolerance and correction in any human activity system can become invalid in the rule-based world of computerized information systems. We simply cannot act fast enough to keep up with the machines, and so instead we often surrender responsibility. But because it is only in hindsight that we can analyse the subtle differences between the dimensions of the human and the computer, there is an enormous potential for misunderstanding. The sheer speed of positive feedback from computers means they are just not in tune with the human mode of error-correction. By our failure to deal with this different time scale, errors are amplified and this feeds back into chaotic situations. Some of the blame for the stock market's Black Monday in 1987 was due to two such problems: first, rapid market fluctuations caused by automatic dealing outpaced the human-scale safeguards; secondly the software itself was programmed with the assumption that it was dealing in a human market with human constraints and reactions, whereas in fact most of the major players in this false market were machines.

We tend to think of communication using machines as an extension of human communication. But adding technology doesn't just make communication more efficient, it makes it different; adding a further complexity. The sender, instead of being in 'writing mode', more often than not is in 'speaking mode'; and the receiver is in the incompatible 'reading mode', and not 'listening mode'. A listener would normally feed back subtle signals that would allow the speaker to adjust his behaviour. However, incompatible modes and the speed at which a complete message can be dispatched deny instantaneous feedback, and no adjustment of the communication is possible. Spontaneous spoken messages are often thoughtless and rash, and can appear rude. Negative feedback is needed so that the message can be qualified, so as not to cause unintentional offence; a feedback that is denied by this technology. Some systems do try to introduce a human dimension to electronic messages, by using different labels for serious messages and for humorous or facetious ones. But this is just another fatuous attempt in IT to reduce the whole spectrum of human subtlety to a bland list of symbols.

Short-term thinking

These differences between human and machine affect the way organizations operate. Even though we have no real perception of the emerging impact of information technology, it is evident that one major effect is the establishment of various forms of short-term thinking. One obvious example is where keen programmers cannot wait to start programming and code is produced rapidly, without the proper preparatory work being done. The resulting inferior programmes bring major maintenance problems, and the necessary on-going repairs can account for over three quarters of programming effort in most organizations. Another phenomenon is that of 'gold-plating'. Programmers want to produce 'all singing, all dancing' state-of-the-art software, even when only straightforward code is requested. The waste of financial resources in this 'overkill' then has a knock-on effect on the long-term profitability of the company that ordered it.

Many of those involved with IT are busy promoting and profiting from it. For example in British universities, the overriding emphasis is on securing funds and sponsorship from industry; business stresses deliverables and products, and any analysis must be 'short, sharp and sweet'. Objectivity is compromised. So it is not surprising that few academics rock the boat of the IT industry, and in the main the cosy myth of strategic competitive advantage, through the application of information technology, goes unchallenged; that is until the flaws can no longer be ignored.

Too many decisions are tactical, relating only to current problems. What is often ignored is the pervasive nature of IT, and how the decisions of today and yesterday create an impetus that will, by default, make the decisions of tomorrow. Many of the monolithic data-processing departments centred around main-frame computers are quite inappropriate in these days of end-user computing; they survive because they have political power; a power founded on the enormous capital expenditure needed to solve the short-term problems of yesterday. At last, many companies are facing up to the pain of writing off huge investments. They recognize the need for a proper understanding of IT for future decisions. However, far too often the people they turn to are the very ones with a vested interest in the status quo.

V

International implications

Given its importance, every country must invest in information technology, and it is essential that we consider the international ramifications of such investment before we can comment on the place of IT in global transition.

The scale of investment will reflect national aspirations, commitment and belief in the ultimate value of information technology. Singapore has probably the most extensive national commitment to date. The prime minister made the strategic decision to charge ahead and transform the whole commercial, legal, governmental and educational infrastructure of the City State, with an ambitious computerization programme. Most other countries are moving more cautiously, and only time will tell if Singapore was right. However, other countries who have travelled this path, but to a lesser extent, have failed. Brazil has drunk from the poisoned chalice of information technology. It attempted to develop an export industry for microcomputers, which it defended at home with import restrictions. The venture, which took an enormous toll on national revenues, collapsed under external pressure from major computer companies. The British government wasted enormous sums when introducing the 'BBC micro' into secondary schools, only to tie the education system into an obsolete technology.

The necessary education and training is very expensive and requires a substantial human infrastructure to support the technology. There is a danger that a country's scarce resources will be used to fund a 'brain drain' that gives advantage to their competitors. Unlike natural raw materials, such expertise can be self-generating, provided a critical mass is maintained. But no country can exist independently of the global economy, and top-quality experts are in great demand. This is the experience of Eire, whose excellent training facilities are supplying the shortfall of experts in Western Europe and the US. Similarly the new-found freedom to travel in Eastern European countries is creating a potential catastrophe for their newly developing market economies. We also have the example of Singapore advertising in Hong Kong in an attempt to attract IT (and other) professionals away, in advance of 1997.

However, satellite communication may be a defence against this parasitical behaviour. Work on IT products does not require the physical presence of the 'knowledge-workers'. This has been recognized by India, and backed by the World Bank, in their strategy to develop 'software factories' aimed at capturing more than ten per cent of the world software market. Thus far they have proved very successful, and they are building up a good reputation for quality and delivery. Also the time difference between India and the US and Europe means that Indian programmers can use expensive state-of-the-art hardware in those countries via satellite for software testing, while the locals are sleeping. But this policy can misfire. A commercially successful package can be produced in one country, but the major profits are made by the marketing company based in a second country; Turbo Pascal was produced in Denmark, and marketed worldwide by Borland

Inc., an American company. Added to this, western companies will expect to pay the 'local rate' for developing countries, and then use these low costs (including minimal transport charges) to force down their expenditure and wage bills at home. This is already the case with data input. Manuel Castells[11] gives an interesting example:

A small Chinese software company finances its development operations by obtaining foreign currency from data entry performed in Beijing for Californian companies... The documents are keyed onto magnetic tape by temporary workers, teenage girls from high schools who are supposed to obtain their 'computer training' through this work for several months, in exchange for a salary equivalent to US$15 per month... The women do not know a word of English, and they transcribe each letter as an ideogramme. The rate of error seems to be lower than in the equivalent operation in the US.

This 'electronic slavery' could be extended so that by the next century, low-level programmers could become the 'car mechanics' of the IT industry. It makes no sense for a country to put all its eggs in one basket by concentrating its resources in producing hordes of low-earning programmers; they must diversify their intellectual resources. India may capture ten per cent of the world software market in volume, but not in income. The global nature of the market, and the fact that communication is a cornerstone of IT, means that no country can isolate itself and still expect to sell internationally. By their very nature, software tools and data artefacts can cross national boundaries instantaneously and unchecked. Even if western companies are willing to pay top prices for these products, the value of a string of binary digits, possibly encrypted, will not be readily apparent to government authorities; rather than bringing 'hard currency' into their home economy, unpatriotic nationals can evade their obligations and invest their income abroad.

But the real money will be made by the 'middlemen', those involved in human communication and situated firmly in the first two stages of our 'information domain', and separated from the production processes of the third stage. Information technology is obviously important, because without it we would have no applications, and no industry. But unless these applications are identified with value-added gains from specific and well-structured solutions to real commercial problems, they will in themselves give little commercial advantage.

VI

It is in information where most investment is being made. Businessmen and politicians, who really should know better, line up to call computer specialists geniuses (see Sir John Harvey-Jones, *Financial Times*, 19 August 1990) or whiz-kids, simply because of their own ignorance of the confusing collection of trivia that makes up so much of information technology. There are far too many inarticulate exponents of low-level IT skills around for them to be credited with the label 'genius'. The present-day short-term skill shortage shrouds the low intellectual content in a mystery that has no inherent value.

The skill that should be valued is the ability to understand and manage the obscurities of applying this technology. Simplistic methodologies of systems development fail to cope with the kaleidoscope of subtlety and intrinsic singularity of a particular business situation. The distinction between the communication of information and its role within control mechanisms has become increasingly unclear. Because of their sheer scale and complexity, international computerized systems can run out of control and so become 'accidents waiting to happen', and it is only a matter of time before misplaced confidence in the merits of IT will be replaced by apprehension about the integrity and security of information systems.

Commercial success is only possible if the industrial and educational infrastructure is expanded beyond the technology. This whole confused and confusing issue will require a strategic stance aimed at minimizing the inevitable risks that surround information technology, whilst making the most of its potential. This strategy must, however, relinquish any expectation of control, even with the methods of 'scientific management'. Fear of this lack of control, and the ensuing insecurity, can drive the terrified businessman into the hands of unscrupulous consultants, sophisters selling 'answers' and certainty. But the problem will not go away, and future success will depend on the right management skills linked to a broad understanding of the place of information systems in both local and global situations. This is only possible by employing the best quality 'thinking managers', who must be thoughtful in, and responsible for, their actions.

It is highly amusing that a technology which, it was claimed, would replace human intellect, turns out to be critically and pivotally dependent on people. The sheer volume and complexity of expertise needed by today's company has culminated in the rise of the 'expert'. Companies that had hoped to reduce their dependence on experts are now more dependent than ever. Experts who are alert to opportunity and have the skills to plan strategically for the future are unwilling to accept conventional wisdom.

These are the experts who not only look forward, but who have developed their powers of hindsight to interpret the past and are the first to take tactical advantage of opportunistic trends they sense around them. This new breed of manager is crucial to the innovation necessary for commercial survival. But innovation is not a secret to be found in text books or high-powered seminars, it is a frame of mind, and the people with the skills to handle this new responsibility are in very short supply. Companies should value this 'social capital', perhaps more than 'financial capital'.[12] Such top-quality human resources do not depend on the accumulation of vocational skills, at best a short-term gain, but on a long-term and continuing invest-ment in education at all levels of management. Vocational skills may be appropriate to the closed technological environment, but it is education that gives an intellectual platform on which to base decisions in these times of change.

So success in information technology means keeping a broad-based edu-cated elite. Neither companies nor countries can afford to lose such valuable assets. High salaries by themselves will not keep them. Those with the 'right stuff' require a stimulating intellectual climate, not a rule-based bureaucracy. They prefer intellectual freedom to organizational constraint and the emphasis must be on human resource management motivating staff to their full potential. Many compromises must be made with present-day 'best practices' in business if the stagnation caused by the loss of good people is to be avoided.

So even with the advent of information technology, nothing has changed. The answer to whether information technology can help transition to a new world order is, as always, 'yes and no'. IT, and in particular telecommuni-cation technology, doesn't necessarily help us maintain a stable infrastruc-ture, for it precipitates further transition, and creates a different infrastruc-ture by changing the ways nations communicate. We cannot control IT, and thus IT cannot control transition. As ever, the availability of good people is the age-old answer. As a tool in the hands of the right people, IT can be an enormous advantage. But forget about the claims of strategic information systems, and don't waste natural intelligence on artificial intelli-gence: as magic wands in the hands of a 'sorcerer's apprentice', they acceler-ate uncontrollable change and bring certain chaos.

References

1. Bell, D., *The Coming of Post-Industrial Society*. New York: Basic Books, 1983
2. Weizenbaum, J., *Computer Power and Human Reason: From Judgement to Calculation*. San Francisco: Freeman & Co., 1976
3. Dreyfus, H. L. and S. E., *Mind over Machine*. Oxford: Blackwell, 1986

4. Liebenau, J., *Medical Science and Medical Industry, Studies in Business History*. London: Macmillan, 1987
5. Ackoff, R., 'Management misinformation systems', *Management Science*, Vol. 14, No. 4, December 1967
6. Parkinson, C. Northcote, *Parkinson's Law*. London: Penguin, 1986
7. Angell, I. O. & S. Smithson, *Management Information Systems: Opportunity or Risk*. London: Macmillan, 1991
8. Marquis, D., *Archy and Mehitabel*. London: Faber and Faber, 1988
9. Straub, B., Ph.D. Thesis, University of London, 1991
10. Liebenau, J. & J. Backhouse, *Understanding Information*. London: Macmillan, 1990
11. Castells, M., *The Informational City*. Oxford: Basil Blackwell Inc., 1989
12. Caruso, R. E., Ph.D. Thesis, University of London, 1990

Ian Angell is Professor and Head of Information Systems at the London School of Economics. He has published ten books and written over sixty papers on research, teaching and commercial interests.

EUROPE AND THE OBSTACLES
TO GLOBAL TRANSITION

Sonya Licht

Were this First International Dialogue being held ten years ago I might have been happy to assert, as someone from Yugoslavia, that my country was Europe in miniature, a laboratory for Europe, and that it seemed to work. Today I have to say that it is indeed Europe in miniature, that it used to be a kind of laboratory, but it seems that it does *not* work. Since I am not a wholly pessimistic person, however, I try hard to analyse why it seems not to have worked, and what I feel are the necessary features to make Europe work as a laboratory for a global society. I shall not say much about Yugoslavia in particular, though it will be in the background of my general discussion.

I

First, I am convinced, partly because of the research in which I am engaged, that for Europe to play an important role in the transition to a global society, it must succeed in preserving its multicultural identity, while at the same time integrating its still diverse elements in a new democratic and non-ideological entity. I emphasize non-ideological, because ideological entities, of which we Eastern Europeans have had more than enough experience, are always imposed from above. And even the best idea, if imposed from above, will very soon become perverted. We have lived through this in Eastern Europe, and we know what we are talking about. In Yugoslavia, multiculturalism – brotherhood and unity, as it was called – was imposed from above, and it failed. Only if the ideas such as multiculturalism, democracy and pluralism come from the grassroots will they have a chance of working creatively. Then they are an expression of people's desire to live together and to retain their identity yet improve their lot.

I agree that unity in diversity is probably the most adequate formula. But how is it to be accomplished when there is still, within Europe, a strong division between the centre and the periphery, when there is a new wave of nationalism, racism, anti-semitism and xenophobia, which is emerging not only in Eastern Europe, not only in Central Europe, but throughout the whole continent? In our part of the world these phenomena are more visible than elsewhere, and are daily threatening to become more dangerous. I would like to say a few words about each of them, but I will start with multiculturalism.

Andrei Cieniawsky, the well-known Russian writer who still lives in exile in Paris, once said in an interview that when he came to Western Europe he was amazed by European diversity, by the differences he found there. 'I was fascinated that it was so different, and it still functions.' This is perhaps one of the best definitions of multiculturalism. And I think that this new kind of multiculturalism, of diverse cultures that work without endangering each other, is the result of a democratic, pluralistic process of development, of tolerance, and of creativity. And for a while these differences really helped a part of Europe to get better and better.

But as I see it, there is one big problem with the multicultural character of Western Europe. It is quite closed with regard to those who are less fortunate, and I think especially of the immigrants, the guest workers, those who came to Europe from elsewhere and who are ready to give to Europe whatever they bring with them of their own cultures. It seems that Europe is quite reluctant to understand and accept these cultures, and that may represent a substantial problem in the future, as far as European multicultural identity is concerned. If only Europeans would be open to these new stimuli, if only they could understand that these people, who by definition are living here still as non-Europeans, will become Europeans, and that they already constitute part of Europe. With such a new understanding, I believe European multiculturalism would be a real transition towards the global community.

These people from the so-called Third World who are coming to Europe are bringing the possibility to those less fortunate Europeans who do not have the opportunity to travel, who perhaps do not therefore understand that they are citizens of the world – and that is the vast majority – to meet these other cultures and to understand them. Of course, all this is taking place in fairly unhappy surroundings. These people are coming to work, to earn a livelihood in Europe. Some of them may not be the best representatives of their respective cultures. But I am convinced that a real openness, a genuinely pluralistic approach, is the way to get the best from these people, and at the same time to make them feel at home in Europe. It is an important and necessary step for European culture in the transition to a global society.

II

The eastern part of Europe, together with the republics of the former Soviet Union, is in a very specific situation. Before the dramatic events of the past few years, Europe sensed the division between the centre and the periphery much less, I think, than it senses it today and will do in the future. I could see this in the interviews that I conducted with intellectuals in Yugoslavia. Prior to 1989, when one spoke about the division between the centre and the periphery, one used to think of the division between the so-called First and Third Worlds. The division between the First and Second Worlds was so completely overshadowed by political and military divisions that nobody, or very few, really thought of Eastern Europe as the periphery. Now the danger is becoming increasingly clear that Western Europe, the United States and other advanced countries such as Japan will form the centre, and that Eastern Europe will remain on the periphery, so we will have this centre/periphery division within Europe itself. It looks as though Eastern Europe is becoming the poor relation of the West. It is therefore necessary, when discussing the transition in Eastern Europe, to take into account some of the very important lessons that have already been learned in the transitions in Latin America.

For years, Eastern Europeans were daydreaming about Europe – to be a European was something so wonderful and still so unreachable. For Western Europeans it was something that was part of their lives, they did not have to think too much about the whole business. To the question: 'Where are the frontiers of Europe?', they answered: 'The Iron Curtain.' Easterners had the same feeling, that Europe begins at the Iron Curtain; but they wanted to cross that bridge, whereas Western Europeans did not, and that was their only wish, to be able to live as people did in the other part of Europe.

Now that we are closer to that possibility, many new problems seem to be coming to light. One of the main problems is that while Eastern Europe may cease to be the poor, so-called socialist part of Europe versus the rich capitalist West, it could well become the poor capitalist part of Europe versus the rich capitalist part. And I am sure that Eastern Europeans would not approve of this kind of development.

How can we overcome this new division, the perpetuation of the division between centre and periphery? I believe that the main way, if not the only one, is for Eastern Europeans to start thinking about the world as a whole; not to do our best to become as the West is already, but to understand that we are all part of one world. We must think in global terms, not because of the others, but because of ourselves and the others.

In Eastern Europe today, I have to say that there is a very strong dislike of the Third World, for many reasons which I cannot go into in this context. The main cause seems to be that for decades they felt that the aid their governments were giving to the Third World was being misused – which was true – and that the powers that be were insisting on this aid for imperial reasons only and not out of solidarity or generosity. Eastern Europeans are also quite frustrated with the Third World because they are afraid of it; afraid that they will soon be in the same position, economically first of all, and perhaps even politically. So it is important to understand these frustrations and not be quick to condemn.

When I recently attended a Peace Convention in Helsinki, I could see how critical the people from the Third World have become towards Eastern Europeans. For example, they are very critical of Hungarians, Poles, Czechs and Yugoslavs who want to go and work in South Africa, who care about nothing except making a living there. These critics need to understand that Eastern Europeans were not brought up to think about the world. If they ever read anything about South Africa, they would say: 'Oh, that's Bolshevik propaganda, its always the same story, who cares?' Because it was a truly totalitarian society that they lived in, not merely one governed by a totalitarian regime, the vast majority developed a one-dimensional view of the world.

III

Now, however, there are real possibilities for developing a new insight. If at least a few people are developing a new openness, they can be the doors by which a message enters and is heard. There is only one problem threatening the success of this message, and that is the resurgent nationalism now rearing its head more and more in Eastern Europe, in fact all over Europe. We are now faced with the emergence of a whole series of nationalist and separatist movements. Many people are convinced that the only path to follow in Europe, and in the global community, is to strengthen their own national and cultural identity. I believe that many of those gathered in these nationalist movements are really rather fearful of the idea of a global community, and even of a united Europe. It was so fascinating to imagine ourselves as being part of that Europe. But now the possibility of fulfilling the dream has arrived, how shall we meet the challenge?

We are only too aware that part of Europe is in many ways more alien than ever, especially in material standard of living, and it is easy to feel that our culture and our identity are somehow endangered. This, I think, is one of the main lines along which the nationalists are thinking. From this it is

a short step to the notion of self-preservation through the further development of the nation-state. Any fostering of the idea and the ideal of the
nation-state – to preserve sovereignty and to control as much territory as
possible – in my view jeopardizes the transition to a new, integrated and
globalized Europe. In any case, there is a contradiction in this desire. If we
want as much territory as possible, how can we be more or less one nation
inside that territory? Instead of thinking in a federalist way, we are thinking
in a nationalist way, and that is why in Eastern Europe – especially Yugoslavia and the former Soviet republics – you hear so much about the
sovereignty of the nation and so little about the sovereignty of the citizen.
The problem is that everybody is longing for a civil society, but with this
insistence on nationality rather than citizenship, political discourse remains
below the level that civil society requires.

I am in no doubt that contemporary nationalism is hostile towards multiculturalism. The nationalists have one main slogan: We are better than the
others and we are endangered by the others. With this slogan you cannot
develop multiculturalism.

Where is the way out? In my view the only way is to strengthen the
independent civil society. One of the prime movers, if not *the* prime mover
of the democratic revolutions of 1989 was the independent civil society.
Unfortunately it seems that it is now in retreat in many of these countries.
One part of it is reflected in the new social movements, the peace movement
and the ecological movement. Unfortunately we have never had a feminist
movement in Eastern Europe, but the good news is that one is starting
now. For obvious reasons the movement for human rights, once very
strong, is less powerful now than it was before. But there are other forms
of independent civil society, and these kinds of discussions and dialogues
are also part of it. They bring people together, and help people to understand that co-operation is the only way to overcome all these threats and
obstacles. It is quite clear that there are people all over Europe who are
aware of the dangers, and who are trying to do something to bring Eastern
Europe closer to Western Europe, and Europe closer to the idea of a global
society.

Sonya Licht studied at Belgrade University and has published numerous
papers on the social and cultural processes of East Central Europe and
Yugoslavia. She is currently a scientific researcher at the Belgrade Institute
for European Studies and has been Workshop Co-ordinator of EUROCIR-
CON since 1988.

TOURISM, CULTURE AND GLOBALIZATION: EUROPEAN PERSPECTIVES

Allan M. Williams

Leisure, recreation and tourism are of central importance to European culture in a number of ways. They are a reflection of the availability of, the use of and the evaluation of leisure time, and recreational opportunities are culturally specific. In addition, tourism is a cultural channel in that it offers the possibilities for cultural interconnections. It makes possible new cultural experiences and cross-border cultural contacts and, therefore, self-education. Furthermore, the influence of tourism can be seen in many areas of economic life, including business activities and the creation of regional images, both of which will be discussed in this paper. The central theme of the paper will be the relationships between tourism, culture and economic development, and the sub-text will be the economics of culture. The paper draws on the current research of EUROCIRCON, on behalf of UNESCO, on the theme of Community, Culture and Development. While the EURO-CIRCON project is concerned with both Western and Eastern Europe, this paper concentrates on the former, given its focus on mass tourism.

I

There are no reliable estimates of the availability of leisure time globally, or of access to tourism and recreation. However, one indicator is the World Tourism Organization estimate that 1,700 million people had the right to paid holidays in the mid-1980s. There are, of course, many people who have access to leisure time without having paid holidays, while many of those with a right to paid holidays lack the means to enjoy recreation or tourism opportunities. Indeed, access to tourism and leisure is socially and regionally varied both within and between countries and continents. One of the most intriguing questions is how this will change during transition to a global society, and what will be the economic and cultural consequences.

It is probably true that the total amount of leisure time available to societies will increase on aggregate. For example, there was a ten per cent reduction in working hours in the European Community during the 1970s.

By 1990, engineers in West Germany were demanding a thirty-five-hour working week, and this seemed likely to become the norm, at least in Northern Europe, especially as the European Community is aiming to establish minimum holiday entitlements and maximum working hours as part of the Social Charter. Reduced working hours do not, of course, translate automatically into increased leisure hours. There are work tasks to be performed at home, and the shift to what Gershuny and Miles[1] term the 'self-service economy' tends to reduce leisure time. Similarly, there has also been a trend in Western and Eastern Europe towards the growth of small firms and self-employment, which are often characterized by a tendency to self-exploitation. More generally, there are persistent differences throughout Europe in the amount of leisure time available to men and women, because of structural inequalities in the household division of labour.[2] For example, in the UK in 1985 the amount of free time available at weekends was 10.2 hours per day for males in full-time employment, 7.2 hours for females in full-time employment and only 5.6 hours for housewives.[3]

Leisure time can be used in many different ways. According to P. E. Murphy,[4] the four main forms are physical (relaxation), social (visiting friends), cultural (learning) and fantasy. Tourism can provide a vehicle for both the cultural and fantasy forms of leisure. As J. Krippendorf writes, increasingly people 'do not feel at ease where they are, where they work and where they live. They need to escape from the burdens of normal life.'[5] Whatever the motive for tourism, there is no denying the remarkable growth of this form of leisure activity, especially in Western Europe. The next section looks at the cultural implications of the growth of mass tourism in Western Europe.

II

Mass tourism: the great cultural robbery

The World Tourism Organization has argued that tourism is an especially 'deep-rooted social custom in European countries'.[6] Such a view does not accord with the history of mass tourism. Until the mid-nineteenth century tourism was essentially restricted to the elites of European societies. Then, in the late nineteenth century, the advent of the railways opened up tourism to the expanding urban middle classes. This was mostly domestic tourism, as resorts such as Estoril and Rothesay grew up to serve, respectively, cities such as Lisbon and Glasgow. There was some international tourism and, for instance, Thomas Cook organized the first international package holidays, being railway-based tours from the UK to the Alps. However, this remained exceptional until well into the twentieth century.

European mass tourism was born only in the 1950s as part of the post-World War II consumer boom. At first this was mostly domestic, but in the 1960s it was to become mass international tourism. On a global scale the rise of international travel is truly impressive. There were twenty-five million international travellers in 1950, 160 million in 1970 and 350 million in 1990 (according to World Tourism Organization reports). Approximately seventy per cent of such travel was for leisure and tourism purposes, and about seventy per cent was also located within Western Europe. Western European dominance of international tourism is not surprising given the spatial conjunction of so many small prosperous countries. Americans travel at least as much and probably more than Europeans, but most of their holiday travels are within the vast expanse of the United States. In contrast, Europe is the world region where international mass tourism is most developed and where, consequently, the opportunities for cultural interconnections and transfers have been greatest. But even in Western Europe tourism, let alone international tourism, is far from universal. In the European Community, for example, only fifty-six per cent of the population takes a holiday away from home, while twenty per cent almost never take such a holiday.[7] Nevertheless, tourism in Western Europe has passed from being a luxury to being a normal privilege or even a basic social right, and some countries already partially recognize this through Social Tourism programmes. It is a question likely to recur in the dialogue about the future form of global transition.

The evolution of mass tourism creates unique opportunities for cultural interchanges and for self-education. M. F. Lanfant, for example, argues that tourism is an 'all-embracing social phenomenon, characterised by the introduction of new systems of relationships . . . bringing about structural changes in all levels of social life.'[8] Yet, in practice, this has not been characteristic of mass tourism in Western Europe. The impact on the receiving countries and on the tourists is little more than skin-deep. Tourism resorts are often exclusive tourist enclaves, purpose-built in accordance with internationalized architectural models. They offer few opportunities for contacts between locals and visitors, and few chances of learning about the life-styles and values of local people. Instead, accommodation and meals are obtained in internationalized restaurants in 'identikit resorts'.[9] Indeed, tourist resorts in the Alps and on the shores of the Mediterranean bear a striking resemblance to colonial enclaves in nineteenth-century Africa, trading in tourists rather than in raw materials. The opportunity for cultural interconnection has been replaced by a largely culturally impoverished mass tourism.

What has brought about the great cultural robbery of the twentieth century? The first clue is provided by the geographical pattern of tourism flows. The dominant feature of mass international tourism is that destinations are located two to four hours' flying time from the major urban population centres. In Western Europe they are largely in the Mediterranean and the Alpine regions. In practice, therefore, the potentially rich variety of cultural interconnectivity is reduced to a small number of international mass flows of tourists.

To some extent this has always been a feature of all forms of tourism. The attractiveness of tourist destinations is partly determined by opinion leaders. Prior to the nineteenth century, royalty and aristocracy set the mark of fashionability on particular resorts. For example, the town of Santander in northern Spain built a summer palace for the royal family, and the esteem that followed led to a major influx of middle-class tourists. In the twentieth century it is film stars and other jet-setters, and travel writers, who define the fashionable and unfashionable resorts.

However, the main mechanism for the great cultural robbery lies in the economics of the tourism industry. Substantial real reductions in the costs of international travel and accommodation have permitted latent demand for mass tourism to be converted into effective demand. This is partly due to the impact of new technology; for example, in 1949 it took eighteen hours to fly the Atlantic but by 1979 this had been reduced to four hours. More importantly, the advent of package holidays sold by tour companies allowed the realization of economies of scale. But tour companies operate almost entirely within national markets and this has important cultural implications. Not least, it means that tourists are channelled into selective resorts depending on the destinations to which national charter airlines fly. For example, Swedish, German and British tour companies all specialize in different Greek-island resorts, which therefore tend to be dominated by tourists from these countries.[10] Similar processes occur elsewhere in the Alps and the Mediterranean, while, within resorts, tourists tend to be segregated into different hotels, apartment blocks or camp-sites.

The net result is that the economics of charter tourism, which permitted the rapid expansion of international mass travel, simultaneously turned it into a culturally introverted process. Many tourists travelled on holidays with, shared hotels with, and mainly interacted with their own national groups. While these closed cultural channels are most characteristic of charter tourists from Northern Europe, they also occur among many other tourist groups. For example, French tourists travelling to Spain are far more likely to use their own cars than to rely on charter aeroplanes. Yet, a large proportion drive directly to the Mediterranean resorts and stay at hotels or camp-sites often dominated by other French nationals. There are, of course, important exceptions; students and young people hitch-hiking around Europe, 'high culture' tourists staying in capital cities, or rural tourists staying on farms all experience far greater opportunities for cultural inter-changes and learning. This is undeniable, but so is the fact of the great cultural robbery of mass tourism.

It can be argued that changes are occurring that will lead to a more culturally aware tourism. There is certainly increased market segmentation, with the development of specific products for particular age groups. There is also an increasingly wide array of destinations available at affordable prices, as well as increasing numbers of activity holidays. Krippendorf[5] is optimistic and sees the emergence of more 'critical consumer tourists', who are more socially, culturally and environmentally aware. While it is certainly true that tourists are demanding higher standards – often in the wake of disasters involving hotels, transport, beaches or ski-slopes – this is not automatically translated into demands for greater cultural content. Instead, demand is likely to be articulated into more golf courses or improved hotel facilities. Most tourists seek out the familiar rather than the new. More critical consumer tourists, therefore, are just as likely to seek out better quality in the familiar mass tourist resorts as they are to seek out opportuni-ties for greater cultural exchanges.

There is also increased product segmentation in the tourist industry, which may offer opportunities for more culturally aware tourism. At the root of this is the fact that the supply of tourist products is not fixed in an absolute sense. Investment can create new tourist attractions and these could provide new models for cultural interaction. In practice, 'high cultural tourism' has tended to be static in recent years. One of the most rapid growth areas, especially in Northern Europe, has been of urban and indus-trial tourism. Nineteenth and early twentieth-century industry and towns have become popular tourist attractions and provide important new forms of cultural tourism.

Modern industry also holds a particular fascination for modern societies and open-days at coal mines, nuclear power stations and so on regularly attract large numbers of visitors. However, the growth of these forms of tourism is from a relatively low base, and will only make a limited impression on the mass tourism market. More typical of the new products of the mass tourism market is the new EuroDisneyland near Paris. Its market is considered to be truly international – those places within two hours' flying time for short weekend breaks – and annual visitor numbers are expected to exceed ten million. If this is the new icon of late-twentieth-century tourism, it is clear that no significant cultural opening can be expected. Mass tourism is more likely to produce a universalization of culturally bland tourism than it is to provide opportunities to learn about the similarities and differences in national cultures.

III

Leisure and business culture

Leisure time is an integral part of life in Western Europe, being formally recognized in national legislation and, for example, in negotiations between employers and employees. The separation of home and workplace that accompanied the advent of urban industrialism and the factory system had a profound effect; with the separation of the places of home and of paid employment (although not of housework) came new forms of time and space constraints on leisure. Leisure hours were regulated by the introduction of formal working hours during the day, week and year. Leisure became more clearly associated with the home, although recreation spaces were often outside the home. To some extent this division has been intensified during the 1970s and the 1980s as more home-orientated, privatized forms of consumption have emerged. For example, video recorders have partly displaced cinemas, and this has relocated some leisure activities from public to private spaces.

One of the features of modern western society has been growing pressures within this arrangement of home and workplaces. The expansion of metropolitan areas, and greater congestion within these, has increased the time and energy resources devoted to linking home and work, that is, to commuting. Sociologists and others have documented the stresses that result in the lives of individuals and their families. This contributed to the 'drop-out' and 'alternative life-style' cultures that have mushroomed in western societies since the 1960s. These can be seen as attempts to develop new ways of linking work and home spaces, thus loosening some of the constraints on leisure and recreation. 'Tele-cottaging' provides one such response, reflecting the increased possibilities for working at home based on information technology applications. Another response has been to establish small firms, often physically located within the home, which offer the possibility of combining work and leisure interests. This merits further consideration as it underlines the increasing influence of leisure and tourism on a number of aspects of contemporary culture, including business culture.

Small firms are a persistent feature of modern economies. Despite the growth of large national and transnational corporations, the majority of firms in most developed countries are small-scale. For example, ninety per cent of firms in Denmark, the Netherlands and Southern Europe employ less than fifty workers.[11] In part, this reflects the emergence of the post-industrial society;[12] there is a shift from manufacturing to service industries and the latter are more likely to be small firms. However, this is not an adequate explanation since, in the 1970s, the share of manufacturing employment in small firms increased in ten out of the twelve current EC states. This phenomenon is explained by reference to a number of factors: a recession leading to firms subcontracting more of their activities in order to reduce costs; technological changes, such as computerized machine tools, which allow smaller-scale and more flexible production; and structural changes such as the growth of real incomes leading to the break-up of mass markets.[13] Another factor, and this is what concerns us here, is socio-cultural change. In short, there is a growing demand in liberal capitalist societies for the status and independence conferred by owning a small firm.

Tourism and recreation are one of the strongholds of small-firm formation in Western Europe. The reasons for this can be understood in terms of the controls on entrepreneurial activity: opportunities, means and motives. Tourism has a positive income elasticity of demand and is one of the most rapidly expanding economic sectors in the developed world. This provides opportunities to establish small businesses. The means required for establishing tourism businesses are modest in terms of previous experience or capital.[14] Establishing a small hotel or cafe requires relatively small-scale initial investment and little working knowledge of such businesses. There are, therefore, low entry barriers into the tourism industry. Finally, the motives for establishing small tourism firms are distinctly socio-cultural, being the search for greater status and independence. In addition, tourism businesses are often viewed by their owners as forms of consumption rather than production. Many of the owners of such businesses in the Mediterranean or the Alps are migrants drawn to these regions as much by the tourist product as by the business opportunities. One study of such firms in Cornwall, England, found that many of the tourism business owners were immigrants from the London region, and their primary motives were to enjoy a more relaxed life-style and an attractive landscape.[14] Such business owners are rarely innovatory, in the sense of the classic entrepreneur. They are risk avoiders rather than risk takers. As such they have much in common with economic traditionalists who view business as a field to be cultivated in the spirit of satisfactory goals.

These inter-regional and, especially, international transfers also contribute to the restrictiveness of cultural channels. British or German tourists in mass tourist resorts on the Mediterranean are often served in bars or housed in hotels owned by their own nationals, rather than by indigenous business owners. We therefore need to be cautious in assuming that small businesses equate in any simply way with cultural diversity, as compared with the supposedly more uniform business culture engendered within transnational companies. There is evidence that the latter is anyway exaggerated.[15]

IV

Regional images and marketing: the role of tourism

Regional images provide another illustration of the importance of leisure and recreation in an increasingly global economy and society. The context for this, at least in Western Europe, has been the gradual withdrawal of the state from regional policy during the 1980s, in response to both the fiscal crises of governments and to the renewed enthusiasm for free-market economics. As a consequence, many regions and communities faced with increasing economic challenges have responded by developing local economic strategies. These tend to emphasize indigenous development and/or self-help,[16] attracting inward investment as well as helping to restore the self-confidence of local economies.

Regional and local imaging is necessarily a selective process, only deploying certain images from the past and the present. For example, the Institute of Culture in Belgrade undertook a study of the regional imaging of the town of Nis. There is a process of symbolic instrumentalism whereby selective use is made of the past to create a modern 'integrative' image of Nis. Literature about the town emphasizes its Roman period when it had positive associations with Constantine the Great, rather than the picturesque medieval or Turkish periods, which stress its provinciality.

Another element in regional imaging is the balance between economic and non-economic elements. If regions are trying to attract inward investment then they must emphasize the availability of economic factors: infrastructure, labour reserves, entrepreneurship, and so on. Yet, given the increasing emphasis on leisure in Western European societies, attention must also be directed at the non-economic aspects of regional life. This is increasingly recognized. A survey of regional imaging in the UK, undertaken as part of the UNESCO project already referred to, found that cultural, social and environmental images were of some importance in the promotional materials of fifty per cent of regional agencies. Even more striking was the fact that these elements were of primary importance in the promotion work of twenty per cent of the agencies. While this is to be expected in the promotion of capital or historic cities, or of beautiful 'unspoilt' rural areas, it is also increasingly evident in the promotion of urban and industrial areas. For example, Knowsley is part of the economically depressed Merseyside region. Yet the introductory section of its promotional literature emphasizes that this is 'a mini-metropolis in its own right, throbbing with life, light-hearted and relaxed – with its own local traditions, local dialect and local humour . . . A borough that cares for its people – with modern houses and schools, museums, libraries and civic centres, elegant restaurants and cosy pubs. Streets for shopping and streets for strolling.'

This type of regional imaging is also writ large into the macro-imaging of the new economic geography of Europe. Sunbelt regions are being promoted in such places as Andalusia, Cambridge, and the South of France. Their attractions include clusters of cultural facilities, of higher educational and research institutes, and agreeable living conditions. Similarly, the projection of the European cities of the future – such places as Lyon or Stuttgart – also emphasizes the special combination of access to new technologies and to leisure facilities alongside the availability of high-tech research and workers.

It is important to consider the cultural implications of such regional imaging. To a considerable extent the regional images are self-fulfilling, especially if they are successful. The regional images will influence the types of public investment undertaken, whether in roads or in cultural facilities. They will also tend to attract certain types of inward investment. This is reinforced by the intense competition that exists between regions to attract inward investment. Simply to create a 'level playing-field' between competing areas, certain investments will be necessary to keep abreast of the advantages offered by other regions. This applies as much to conference centres and concert halls as to airports and IT. There are therefore certain homogenization tendencies inherent in the process of regional imaging. This is most strikingly evident in the post-modernist architecture that decorates the growing number of rejuvenated waterfront areas in Europe's larger cities.

V

Globalization and tourism and leisure

The process of globalization does not occur against a colourless background. Existing structures condition the possibilities for change; in other words, structure and process are interlinked. This applies as much to the cultural aspects of tourism and leisure as to the employment effects of economic changes. Existing patterns of tourism and leisure have created built forms in bricks and concrete. These represent fixed capital as well as fixed interests, which will only change slowly even in the increasingly rapid process of globalization.

Despite these reservations, tourism offers great opportunities in the process of globalization. Mass tourism is, in essence, a closed cultural channel, but there are other forms of tourism. Business tourism, 'back-pack' tourism and individual travel all offer opportunities for self-education, and for greater awareness of the similarities and diversity within cultures. Above all, it provides insights into how people live, the challenges that face them and their responses to them. The hope must be that mass tourism – or substitutes for it – will, in future, encourage this greater cultural openness. The importance of this openness should not be underestimated. In an age when there is little serious reading and people are becoming immune to the images presented on their television and video screens, tourism may provide an increasingly important means of raising awareness of the global challenges that now face us and require global responses.

References

1. Gershuny, J. I. and I. D. Miles, *The New Service Economy*. London: Frances Pinter, 1983
2. Pahl, R. E., *Divisions of Labour*. Oxford: Basil Blackwell, 1984
3. Hudson, R. and A. M. Williams, *Divided Britain*. London: Frances Pinter, 1989
4. Murphy, P. E., 'Perceptions and attitudes of decision-making groups in tourism centres', *Journal of Travel Research*, Vol. 21, pp. 8–21, 1982
5. Krippendorf, J., 'The new tourist turning-point for leisure and travel', *Tourism Management*, Vol. 7, pp. 131–5, 1986
6. World Tourism Organization, *Economic Review of World Tourism*. Madrid: World Tourism Organization, 1984
7. Commission of the European Communities, *Europeans and their Holidays*, VII/165/87-EN, Brussels, 1987
8. Lanfant, M. F., 'Introduction: tourism in the process of internationalisation', *International Social Science Journal*, Vol. 23, pp. 14–43, 1980
9. Holloway, J. C., *The Business of Tourism*. London: Macdonald and Evans, 1983
10. Pearce, D. G., 'Mediterranean charters – a comparative geographic perspective', *Tourism Management*, Vol. 8, pp. 291–305, 1987
11. Williams, A., *The Western European Economy*. London: Hutchinson, 1987
12. Bell, D., *The Coming of Post Industrial Society*. London: Heinemann, 1974
13. Mason, C. M. and R. T. Harrison, 'Small firms: phoenix from the ashes?', in D. Pinder (ed.), *Western Europe: Challenge and Change*. London: Frances Pinter, 1990
14. Williams, A., Shaw, G. and J. Greenwood, 'From tourist to tourism entrepren-

eur, from consumption to production', *Environment and Planning A*, Vol. 21, pp. 1639–1653, 1989

15. Mole, J., *Mind Your Manners*. London: Industrial Society Press, 1990
16. Bassand, M., Brugger, E. A., Bryden, J. M., Friedmann, J. and B. Stuckey, *Self-Reliant Development in Europe*. Aldershot: Gower, 1986

Allan Williams is Co-Director of the Western European Studies Centre at the University of Exeter, UK. His main research interests are uneven development and the transformation of Southern Europe, the Western European economic transition, and tourism and recreation.

PERSPECTIVES, PURPOSES AND BROTHERHOOD: A SPIRITUAL FRAMEWORK FOR A GLOBAL SOCIETY

John Huddleston

I

In discussing a new vision and new values for an emerging world order, we might define vision as a spiritual insight of who we are, why we are, and where we are going. Values might be similarly defined as standards of spiritual worth by which we try to live in accordance with our vision. A society needs vision because it is a powerful motivator for forward movement; conversely in the absence of vision a society can slip backwards towards disintegration. 'Where there no vision, the people perish.'[1]

A variation on this theme is the perception that a vision, like a strategic plan, helps a society to be more efficient and effective, because it provides a sense of direction, and thereby reduces the risk of inconsistencies and error. A good example of a need for such a vision or plan today is, as Henry Kissinger has pointed out, with regard to the whole process of disarmament: we need to know where are trying to go. Clearly such needs are of particular significance in times of rapid and radical change.

II

For most of history since the beginning of civilization and for the vast majority of humanity, vision and values have been intimately associated with the religious experience. Religion has presented a vision of a time when righteousness shall prevail (the coming of the New Jerusalem) and when there will be universal peace: 'They shall beat their swords into ploughshares, and their spears into pruning hooks. Nation shall not lift up sword against nation, neither shall they learn war any more.'[2]

Such a time is usually connected in the human mind with the coming or return of a Manifestation or Messenger of God: The Second Coming of Christ, the Messiah, the Fifth Buddha, Shah Bahram, the Q'aim, the Mihdi, and so on. The deep values promulgated by the great religions have over and over again helped to propel civilization forward, ranging from ancient times when biblical prophets held up an independent system of morality against which to measure the activities of the state, to modern times when religious inspiration largely caused the abolition of slavery and gave great strength to the movement for human rights. However, it is undoubtedly true that in modern times, and especially in the West, established religion has lost much of its attraction. As is true of all living things, religions have a life cycle and with age they become corrupted with superstition, fanaticism, hypocrisy, division and oppression. Disillusioned, humanity has searched for inspiration in alternative secular philosophies.

III

One of the great forces of modern times that has captured the imagination of millions is democratic capitalism. In reaction to the suffocating effects of mercantilism and absolute monarchy, legitimized as the viceroyalty of God, democratic capitalism has held up a vision of maximum freedom for all: political, economic and social. The goal has been to maximize human happiness. As Bentham put it: 'The greatest happiness of the greatest number is the foundation of morals and legislation.'

As each person is the best judge of what makes him or her happy, clearly the optimum social system is one that, within the bounds of maintaining basic law and order, maximizes individual freedom. Unfortunately all men and women are not born equal and maximum freedom tends to make differences more extreme and, in particular, to cause, on the one hand, many to be deprived of the basic economic necessities, and on the other hand, a few to have excess of power and influence.

And so we have, in reaction to the gross and obvious inequalities of early democratic capitalism, the emergence of a new socialist 'vision': an egalitarian society where there would be no poverty and no dominating rich. There were, of course, many variations on the socialist theme: co-operatives, trade unionism, anarchism, syndicalism and so on, but the one that became predominant was characterized by the highly centralized control of a bureaucratic state, with the Stalinist model being the most extreme example. This vision has failed, as we have all recently witnessed.[3] Beyond a certain point central control did not lead to economies of scale but rather to rigidities and reduced initiative and incentive. In extreme cases the system became highly efficient and failed to create the additional wealth needed to raise everyone from poverty. Furthermore, those in control for too long apparently thought that they alone were exempt from Lord Acton's dictum: 'Power tends to corrupt, and absolute power corrupts absolutely.'

Talk about a new Soviet Man first became a bad joke and then simply stopped. No wonder Vaclav Havel has felt compelled to say: 'Let us teach both ourselves and others that politics . . . can be the art of the impossible, that it is the art of making both ourselves and the world better.'

And so it seems that democratic capitalism is triumphant. After successes in Latin America, East Asia, and Southern Europe over the past decade or so, we have just witnessed amazing advances in Eastern Europe and the countries of the former Soviet Union. For the first time in history, democracies, in the loosest sense, may be a majority of the world's nations. As a jewel in the crown, we have a strengthened European Community and the promise of further European integration. The question now is: does democratic capitalism provide, after all, the vision and values needed for a new world order? Clearly there are positive things that can be said. For instance, it is argued from experience that democracies rarely instigate a war, and certainly their record in this respect is better than that of authoritarian regimes. Second, it is fair to assume that evolution of international co-operation towards a federal world government is much more likely to happen if the majority of the member nations of such an organization are democratic, follow the rule of law in domestic affairs, and are accountable to their citizens.

However, I would suggest that democratic capitalism is essentially hollow at the centre in the same way as socialism, and accordingly, its vision and system of values is inadequate for our time. The system lacks a soul. It rests on the assumption that man differs from animals only because of his superior intelligence. Bentham's 'happiness' fundamentally means material enjoyment and consumption. Indeed, we are proud of the fact that ours is a consumer society. But there is growing fear that the earth will not be able to sustain a world society where five billion persons would consume material things at the same rate as the one billion persons who presently live in economically developed nations. There is also growing recognition that when the goal of life is 'happiness' there will always be frustration. Once the materialist philosophy seemed sunny and optimistic; but experience in the twentieth century and the prevailing sense of frustration has made for pessimism, and today any self-respecting man of the world has to sound sceptical if not cynical. We now see humanity as essentially selfish, greedy and violent; hardly a view that will encourage the building of a new world. Furthermore, there is an inexorable logic in the materialistic view that drives it towards a short-term perspective: 'for tomorrow we die'. And yet vision has always been about the long-term perspective. I do not mean to exaggerate or imply that all democracies are exactly the same. But I suggest there is an underlying trend that can be clearly seen, for instance, in the United States, the most powerful democracy and the one that is increasingly a model for the rest of the world.

IV

Let me list a few characteristics of modern American society that are common knowledge. First, in politics it is obvious that the horizon of vision is essentially limited by the next congressional or presidential election. President Bush speaks disparagingly about 'this vision thing'. It is the Senate of this nation that voted against ratification of the League of Nations Covenant, and for forty years refused to approve the International Genocide Convention. Though there is apparently free public discussion, the reality is that voting and decision-making are largely responsive to rhetoric and TV 'sound-bites'. Wealth, both corporate and private, has an immense influence that it uses for its own perceived vested interest, and this frequently does not coincide with the general public good. The advice of Edmund Burke to representatives of the people, that they put the nation first, is largely ignored, and parochialism is what counts. Thus political favouritism dominates the Federal Budget. The economy is likewise preoccupied with short-term considerations, as epitomized by obsession with the price/earnings ratio in quarterly corporation reports. Takeover merchants buy and sell large corporations with borrowed money and show little concern for either employees or customers, whilst more people are obliged to live on the streets. Saving rates in this, the richest country in the world, are at an all time low; conversely debt, private, commercial and public, continues to rise for the financing of consumer goods and services rather than for investment in productive resources. Maintenance of the basic infrastructure of education, health, housing and communications is neglected. There is powerful inertia resisting attempts to protect natural resources and a healthy environment, as symbolized by the absurdly low tax on gasoline. In the social sphere there is the devastation of the family, routine divorce for all and abandonment of children; the result is good money for the psychiatrist and a culture of alcohol, drugs, guns, violence, racism and crime. My purpose in recounting this tale of woe is not to put down the country where I live or democratic capitalism in general, but rather to show that we need more lofty standards if we are to start to build a true world order for succeeding generations.

Ah, but a man's reach should exceed his grasp,
Or what's a heaven for.[4]

If indeed the materialistic dreams of socialism and democratic capitalism are inadequate, the logical question to ask is whether we should take another look at the religious experience, the main source of vision and ethical values down the ages. Many thinkers of modern times, as diverse as Toynbee, Koestler and Campbell have come to this conclusion. An intuitive sense of the correctness of this view is supported by popular feeling in Eastern Europe where there has been a new reaching out for the spiritual dimension despite decades of state-directed suppression of religion. Similarly there is a reaction in the Islamic world against the corruption of western material-ism. It is perhaps not irrelevant to observe that about eighty per cent of the world's population still claims religious affiliation.[5] What seems to be needed is a focus on the essence of the vision: relevant universal themes that are common to all the great religions. I wish to stress my view that such a focus on the inspirational essence of religion is very different from conventional ecumenicalism, which so often ends in the dreary lowest common denominator.

V

I would suggest there are at least five universal religious themes relevant to this discussion. The first is an awareness of a spiritual dimension to life and existence as well as a material dimension. A consequence of such an aware-ness is that material things become less important and are viewed as of temporary interest. This does not mean indifference or asceticism but rather a balance, a golden mean – an enjoyment of the material creation but a detachment and a willingness to let go when the time comes.

This leads to a second key theme, namely a sense of the sacredness, interdependence and harmony of life. Hubris, which the Greeks so feared, can hardly exist when there is such an awareness. At the same time, balan-cing this humility, is a self-esteem that comes from the belief that man is the highest form of life, not simply because of his superior intelligence, but because he has a consciousness of the transcendental, and a spiritual side to his nature. He is, in essence, made in the image of God. From this privilege comes an acknowledgement of responsibility, including account-ability for the stewardship of the earth. Linked to this perspective is a fourth theme, which is recognition that the purpose of life is to nurture and develop the spiritual side of our nature; to cultivate the noble qualities: truthfulness, honesty, courage, reliability, compassion, courtesy and so on. This purpose is different from the utilitarian idea of 'happiness', because, though it can indeed bring in its wake intense happiness and a sense of fulfilment, the path to it is often through pain and sacrifice.

Man is, so to speak, unripe; the heat of the fire of suffering will mature him. Look back to the times of the past and you will find that the greatest men have suffered the most.[6]

A fifth theme of religion, closely linked to the other four, is an insistence on the fact that we are all Children of God – the human family. This theme is relevant at every level of society, from humanity as a whole down to its basic building block: the family.

When such themes are taken seriously, the consequences for a new world order are potentially immense. A feeling of human solidarity is the most powerful base for international co-operation and ultimately for a world government. That same solidarity makes it impossible to be indifferent to poverty among our brothers and sisters of the same race, whether living within one's own country or elsewhere. A focus on our spiritual development as the highest priority, a detached and balanced attitude towards material goods, and a feeling of respect for nature, are all factors that lead humanity towards a vastly enhanced concern for the protection of natural resources and the environment. There is a basis here for a new-style global economy that benefits all by putting emphasis on basic material needs and on high-quality services designed to enrich the general intellectual and spiritual experience. An emphasis on development of noble qualities also has implications for a higher level of honesty and efficiency in both the public and the private sectors. We in the West are perhaps conscious of this issue because of our experience, over several decades, of a decline in ethical standards simultaneously with a decline in religion. It is suggested that in the long term these goals, together with support for the family as one of the most vital institutions of society, represent the most effective way to reverse the devastating trend towards drugs, crime, and other symptoms of social breakdown.

VI

The potential value of focusing on the essence of the religious experience suggests the need for radical change if we are to achieve a solid base from which to move forward to a new world order. First, there is a need for the leaders of religions to join together for the common good, an action that can only strengthen rather than undermine the religious tradition they love.

The challenge facing the religious leaders of mankind is to . . . submerge their theological differences in a great spirit of mutual

forbearance that will enable them to work together for the advancement of human understanding and peace.[7]

Second, there is a need for global action on the part of government and
education authorities to incorporate into the education system the basic
spiritual insights of religion. This should surely be given the same order of
priority as the elimination of illiteracy. In the United States such an idea
may sound shocking, because the public education authorities, particularly
in recent decades, have made almost a fetish out of excluding any mention
of religion from the syllabus. There is fear that otherwise they could be
accused of acting in contravention of a constitutional requirement for separation of Church and state. However, there is a need to look at the motives
behind that requirement. It is clear that the Founders were generally
religious in outlook and did not intend to make the new nation atheistic;
their concern was to make sure that a particular denomination did not use
the state to force its views on a multicultural society whose peoples had in
many instances fled Europe on account of an unholy authoritarian alliance
of Church and state. The proposal made here would not contradict that
objective and at the same time would avoid the terrible price that American
society has had to pay as a result of present policies.

But the religious experience offers more than a basic foundation for a
new vision and a related system of values, important as that undoubtedly
is. In its modern manifestation, religion also presents a framework or super-
structure around which humanity can build a new global society of peace
and justice. This framework is a logical development of the basic universal
themes, adapted to the special needs of a world maturing towards a global
society.

A major element of this vision is a new system for management of
public affairs, based on participatory local community government, and
culminating, through national bodies, in a federal world government. The
approach is to go beyond the democratic system of election by confidential
universal suffrage, public accountability, free public discussion, and the rule
of law, to a system incorporating several new principles of which perhaps
the two most important are a spiritual dimension, and a process of consultation rather than democratic debate. The spiritual dimension includes a
requirement that those casting a vote in an election take account of spiritual
or noble qualities as well as administrative capacity. It also means that
elected government is responsible first to God rather than to the electorate.
In practice, this means a holistic viewpoint, embracing not only the interests
of the present but of the future, and of the environment as well as humanity.
It means a focus on creating conditions that maximize opportunity for

every man, woman and child on the planet to develop his or her full potential, physical, intellectual, and above all, spiritual. One aspect of this process is a style of government that is collective rather than dependent on the individual leader; a change designed to avoid the corruption that the latter role inevitably entails. The process of consultation differs from democratic debate insofar as it aims to arrive at the truth through unity and a scientific process rather than through conflict and appeal to self-interest. This process involves both detachment and universal participation. It is akin in many ways to current ideas on conflict resolution.

This vision of a new way of managing public affairs is intimately related to a refined and heightened awareness of the basic universal religious themes. Thus, in promoting the idea of the human family there is an emphasis on conscious abolition of prejudice and appreciation of the diversity of culture as a means for enriching the common heritage. These are critical nuances in a world where migrations, international trade and tourism bring us into contact more and more with peoples who are very different from ourselves. This theme of the oneness of humanity is reinforced by practising the equality of men and women within the family and in society in general. Many see the latter process as vital to the establishment of peace because of the special perspective that women generally have on the priorities of society. This theme of oneness is further strengthened, as is a sense of responsibility and accountability, by the viewpoint that the highest form of worship is work in the service of humanity. Finally, the universal religious theme of detachment, which counters the materialistic drive towards conflict, is sharpened by the encouragement of intellectual integrity and independent investigation of truth and by the view that science and religion, dealing respectively with the material and the spiritual dimensions of existence, are in harmony, not conflict.

VII

A vision, to have reality, must surely incorporate some indication of how we get from here to there. This too can be found in the vision of religion in its modern form. It starts at the grassroots level with the individual and the local community gradually creating an alternative working model, initially on a small scale, of a diverse society with a global perspective. It continues with a reaching out to other groups and organizations that have goals fitting into the global vision, all with a view to mutual co-operation for the common good. A global perspective means avoidance of entanglements with partisan and parochial interests, and this, when combined with the principle of loyalty to established government, creates a sense of trust, a key factor in building a new world society. One of the most important stages on the way to the establishment of a world commonwealth based on justice and spiritual values is the abolition of war between nations, a stage that should be achieved by the end of this century.

To summarize, finding a new vision and an associated new system of values is a vital component of the process of evolving towards a peaceful global society. It is suggested that in searching for such a vision, there should be an objective analysis of what is offered by religious experience: the source of the great visions of the past.

References
1. Proverbs 29:18
2. Isaiah 2:4
3. Though the failure has been most dramatic in the communist countries it should not be forgotten that in the West the welfare state, even in model Sweden, has been under siege for a decade on such issues as efficiency, dependency culture and so on.
4. Robert Browning, 'Andrea del Sarto'.
5. See 'Religion: World Religious Statistics', Britannica Book of the Year, 1988
6. 'Abdu'l-Bahá, Paris Talks. London: UK Bahá'í Publishing Trust, 1969
7. The Universal House of Justice, The Promise of World Peace. London: Oneworld Publications, 1985

John Huddleston has been working for the International Monetary Fund, Washington, DC since 1963. He was the Chief of the Budget and Planning Division from 1977 to 1986, and is currently the Assistant Director of the Administration Department.

GLOBAL UNITY AND THE ARTS

Kathleen Raine

I

We have listened, during these days of intense thought, to many world-famous authorities on the natural and social sciences, and we have heard them speak of the scientific and technological means now available for the transmission of information linking the whole planet in 'global unity'. But I am here to speak for the poets, and poetry is the language not of quantifiable and computable fact, but of the soul, whose meanings and values are immeasurable. And I have found myself wondering what is the use of all these communication techniques, interdisciplinary dialogues, satellite transmission of instantaneous information to myriad television sets all over our planet, indeed of that much-vaunted and unchallenged activity 'education' itself, unless we address ourselves to a question raised here by John Huddleston and Professor Bushrui.

That question is the oldest in the world: 'What is Man?'

The answer Oedipus gave to the Sphinx's riddle about 'Four legs, two legs, three legs' is surely simplistic. So natural man may be defined, as T. S. Eliot reminded my generation when he wrote that 'life on a crocodile-isle' is 'just three things: Birth, and copulation, and death'. But the Hebrew psalmist's cry to God,

> What is man, that thou art mindful of him?
> And the son of man that thou visitest him?
> For thou hast made him a little lower than the angels
> And hast crowned him with glory and honour

concerns man as a living spirit, a mystery.

William Blake, our English poet-prophet, also asked the question, and his answer was: 'Man is either the Ark of God, or a phantom of the earth and of the water.' To Blake, man is without doubt the bearer of the divine presence. Again in this century, Rabindranath Tagore, in one of his last poems, 'The Rising Sun', puts the question to man: 'Who are you?' Tagore gives no answer, for indeed man is rooted in mystery: not only unknown but unknowable.

This at least we know, that humanity cannot be defined or described in material terms or in terms of quantity. Measurement cannot discover the immeasurable. The power that moves the sun and the other stars lies altogether outside the order of materialistic science and its child, technology. I quote again from William Blake:

> Every natural effect has a spiritual cause,
> And not a natural. A natural cause only seems.

And I ask again: What is the use of more and more communication systems, universal literacy and the rest, unless we know whom we are educating and for what end? I am reminded of some lines by T. S. Eliot, from *The Waste Land*:

> I can connect
> Nothing with nothing.

Technology, whose 'medium is the message', so we have been told, can only connect 'nothing with nothing'. All those international and interdisciplinary exchanges, all that instantaneous flashing of information on TV screens across the globe is futile unless there is a reconnection with the lost source.

In the context of a culture built on the premise that the ground of reality is 'matter', the arts can only be cosmetic, a coating of pink icing to sweeten harsh reality: classes in 'creative writing' and everyone 'doing their own thing', indulging in harmless pastimes while the scientists and technicians decide the 'real' issues. This widespread and popular concession to 'human values' and 'the arts' has been described by C. S. Lewis as 'making mud-pies'. Yet until relatively recently every human civilization since the dawn of time had been based on the recognition that the ground of reality is spirit. The world's great heritage of knowledge and wisdom, of philosophy and the arts, is grounded in this premise. Ours is an imaginatively and spiritually illiterate culture that no longer takes values and meanings seriously, nor gives Plato's inner realities of the good, the true and the beautiful one fraction of the attention given to technological inventions.

There has been much talk of 'new values'. But reality is always itself; there is already a great treasury of knowledge and wisdom, which is only rendered irrelevant, and excluded, by materialist science. It is not the *conclusions* of this materialist science that we must question, however, but the *premises*.

II

We are a centrifugal society, seeking to join together pieces of the fragmented periphery, when 'the centre cannot hold'. Unless that lost centre, that dimension opening into eternal, immeasurable worlds, is restored, all these peripheral connections of 'nothing with nothing' can only result in a global unity that is bleak indeed. I offer a few very simple thoughts on the necessity of the arts of the imagination as one means of restoring the lost dimension. These thoughts may be considered almost too simple and self-evident; yet truth may often elude us by its very simplicity.

The simple truth is that there is one sphere in which there is no need for a 'transition' to a global society. For that society is already here, has been from the beginning and will be always: that is, the world of the arts of the imagination. Of that 'kingdom not of this world', all are citizens who choose to enter its regions. In the 'realms of gold' where the poet John Keats had 'so many goodly states and kingdom seen', there are no frontiers, and no conflicts. Within that world there is no competitive struggle for possession because there is no property; all belongs to everyone, like the light of the sun.

The nature of property is a principal cause of conflict and division in the material world. For only one person, or group of persons, or nation, can possess a piece of land or other form of wealth, to the exclusion of others. If a sum of money is shared by a hundred people, each receives only a hundredth part. In the world of the arts of the imagination, the opposite is true: if a hundred people listen to a symphony by Schubert or a play by Shakespeare, or visit some cathedral, mosque, or temple, or memorize a psalm or sonnet, each one of that hundred possesses the whole undiminished by no matter how many other participants. The capacity of a concert-hall or theatre may be limited, but the music or poetry itself is not. The world of Homer, or Valmiki, or Shakespeare, or Proust, or Shelley, or Tagore, can be ours totally, according to our capacity, with added delight because these worlds are also shared by many others.

The principle is a very simple one: the greater the numbers in the material world, the more human beings fear, mistrust and compete with one another. In that other world, far from separating the many who participate in music, drama, poetry, or whatever art, all are united in a bond of shared knowledge and delight in a single imaginative experience. And what is a civilization if not the participation of many in certain shared imaginative regions? We live not only in houses of stone, but also in regions of the mind. Because the imagination is universal, the vision of one, given its fitting form, thereby becomes 'the house of the soul', a description the Cambridge scholar I. A.

Richards used of poetry. There is no limit to how many can dwell in such a house.

III

Each nation, or tribe, has its own imaginative identity; indeed it is certain shared modes of expression, or melodies, stories, dance or other arts, that above all unite tribe or nation. From a material standpoint, what is England but a small, overcrowded island with a wet climate and an industrial economy? But what of the England of the imagination? What would England be without her poets, without Shakespeare, and our theatre, without our Gothic cathedrals? The England of the imagination belongs to the whole world; and there is an Ireland, a France, a Germany, an Italy, an India, a China, a Japan, an America, a Russia of the imagination. Citizenship is a privilege more or less jealously guarded by national governments. But the vast landscapes of French literature, German music, the treasures of Greece and Italy, are open to the whole world. There are no frontiers, not even between nations that are politically very hostile to one another. We too may possess dual or multiple citizenship if we so wish. All may be fellow-citizens of the one world of the imagination; we are in some measure already citizens of any country whose arts we love and have become part of our being.

In the West and in the westernized modern world, we live under the domination of a materialist ideology that has prevailed since the seventeenth century. None can know the ultimate nature of reality, but as we believe it to be, so our belief becomes an agent in creating a certain kind of world. Materialist ideology rests, as I have said, on the hypothesis that matter is the basis of reality and that it exists independently of mind or thought. This belief has created a lifeless universe, to be known by weight and measure, infinitely divisible but devoid of qualities, of meanings and values; devoid of life. The inevitable result is that human meanings and values appear insubstantial, irrelevant, less real than the many ingenious products of technology.

This material system, regarded virtually throughout modern westernized society as the whole and only reality, envisages a world made up of an infinite number of parts, divisible *ad infinitum*, not a unity but a multiplicity, a fragmentation. Individuals, like nations, each seek to possess as much of the property to be divided as possible; all is partitioned and 'owned'. A materialist civilization is inevitably self-destructive in the long run because it is so divisive and competitive. Nor is a materialist egalitarianism any solution, for an equal division is no less a division than an unequal

one. England's great visionary poet William Blake understood these things
as early as the end of the eighteenth century, a time when materialist science
was already in the ascendant:

> More, more, is the cry of a mistaken soul.
> Less than all will not satisfy man.

Imagination, the world of mind and spirit, is by its nature a unity, a universe
of sacred values and meanings, of joys and sorrows, whose reality does not
depend on any hypothesis about 'matter'; whereas in the world of materialist science, where reality is equated with what can be measured and quant-
ified, nothing is sacred. Again, the contrast is highlighted by Blake; to the
follower of a materialist science who asked him 'When the sun rises, do
you not see a round disk of fire, somewhat like a guinea?' he replied: 'Oh
no, no, I see an innumerable company of the heavenly host, crying "Holy,
holy, holy".'

Over the years I have come to realize that the crisis of these times can
be resolved by nothing less than a change in the premises of our civilization.
W. B. Yeats, in his book *A Vision*, set forth a paradigm of the historic
cycles, in which world civilizations succeed one another. He too proclaimed
a New Age. 'The three provincial centuries are over', he wrote to a friend,
'wisdom and poetry return'. Poetry is the language of wisdom, which
belongs to the spirit, to the imagination, not to a science of quantification
and a technological civilization. The prophecies of Blake, Shelley, Yeats and
other poets are self-fulfilling.

Must we not have more cultural exchanges between nations? Yes, but
what culture is to be exchanged? Exchange is of no avail unless it be at the
level of the unifying imagination. For this the participants themselves must
possess such a culture of the imagination. This may be a traditional culture,
like that of India, or a learned tradition, like that of pre-war Europe, based
on a high degree of literacy. Where are we to turn in a new post-literate
world?

IV

No true cultural exchange can take place unless the education of the imagination is first established. Those who are responsive to works of the imagination within their own culture will naturally bring the same response to
other cultures. The widespread advance of technological education throughout the world cannot bring about global unity, only global uniformity.
Unless we provide a different education, the education of the imagination,

that world will remain closed, and competitive acquisitiveness will continue to prevail.

In speaking of the imagination we are not appealing to an elite such as the elite of science, comprising those who are exceptionally gifted and highly trained in some special field of knowledge. We are speaking of universal human nature, the great human family. The shared vision of Christendom once gave a unity of imaginative culture to Europe, for the great 'revealed' religions are traditionally vehicles for a collective imaginative vision, giving stability and coherence. But they remain so only as long as that informing vision is not obscured by attempts to manipulate a vision of higher things for worldly ends. Are not the world's religions themselves at this time in dire need of imaginative renewal?

Unfortunately, modern education tends to be utilitarian and technological. With this kind of education, a nation's imagination is no longer sustained by some shared mythology or poetry. But the loss of such cultural unity can destroy a civilization more speedily than the imagination can build it. How can we restore that unity? What is the new education that can give back to a new generation that lost kingdom?

World-wide dissatisfaction with the materialist values that seek to feed humankind with 'bread alone' is perhaps already creating its own antidote: there is a deep need, a universal search for the lost values of the spirit. I can speak only for my own *Temenos* circle in England, at present working towards the establishment of a Temenos Academy of Integral Studies, which will seek to plant a seed of what may be the education of the future: an education grounded in perennial wisdom, which alone can bring about global unity at the level of humankind's highest vision and deepest understanding. There are other movements in other parts of the world, inspired by the same need. Yet once a culture has been lost, a continuity broken, might it not be impossible to restore it? If we act now, we may be just in time to save our rich heritage of the treasures of the imagination.

The human imagination itself, of course, is always there. Yet we also need the works of the imagination hitherto preserved in all cultures, which constitute the language of every nation's experience. They are the means whereby we learn from the past, from our ancestors, and communicate with future generations.

It is for this reason that I speak for the arts, for language itself, through which alone we partake of what the Christian scriptures call 'the gifts of the spirit'. The universe of the imagination, for those who participate in it, remains a living unity in an ageless, deathless world with no frontiers, embracing past and future alike in the only universal reality, our shared vision of eternity.

Kathleen Raine is the foremost contemporary woman poet writing in English. She is the editor of the influential *Temenos Review* and is considered to be the leading authority on Blake and Yeats in the English-speaking world.

SUMMARY OF PROCEEDINGS

The First International Dialogue on the Transition to a Global Society was a five-day conference that attracted a broad cross-section of speakers and deliberated on a number of important topics. For the purposes of this book, several of the contributions have had to be excluded owing to constraints on length. Every effort has been made, however, to offer a collection showing the diversity and breadth of viewpoints expressed at the conference. The following summary of the full proceedings is intended to give readers an idea of the scope and something of the flavour of the First International Dialogue.

SUMMARY OF PROCEEDINGS

James Malarkey

Day One
Tuesday 4 September 1990

OPENING SESSION

Iraj Ayman reaffirmed the mission of the dialogue: to develop a coherent vision of the future, to share this message with the rank and file, and enlist collaboration, especially of managers and young people.

The organizers envisage creating a new association to carry forward the study of the transition to global society.

Prince Alfred of Liechtenstein identified seven key global issues – demography, environment, energy, urbanization, economic systems, presentation of cultural diversity, and collective security – indicating that interdisciplinary approaches and teamwork are rare but badly needed. The Vienna Academy is showing leadership in this area at the graduate level.

Murray Polakoff reminded us that over 100 states are currently involved in conflict. The sense of hopelessness among the young is disturbing and youth are likely to grow more cynical as natural resources become depleted and environmental pollution increases. He agreed with Prince Alfred that the organization of higher education into departments has inhibited the integration of knowledge and action. The Center for International Development and Conflict Management at the University of Maryland is an effort to overcome this problem, since it is interdisciplinary and holistic in orientation.

Wolfgang Blenk argued that we need to rationalize our efforts in order to deal with global problems. However, we are confronted with uncertainty in virtually every area: in nature (which is too complex to predict); science (evidenced by frequent disagreement); in planning (the effects of which are often debatable); in economics (since the variables and priorities are hard to define); in politics (since goals are in dispute).

We are faced with the fact that we must make decisions and act even if we cannot predict with precision what the outcome will be. Blenk concluded that despite the uncertainties, we clearly must aim for sustainability. 'Continuity of life on earth must be central to spirituality, a new morality or trusteeship.'

In the discussion, Karan Singh and Suheil Bushrui questioned whether rational efforts would be sufficient to solve our problems. Irrational forces, both for good and evil, threaten us from all directions. Pentti Malaska indicated that an issue the Prince failed to mention was the problem of how to view life as a whole, and how to learn from nature's non-polluting ways of solving problems.

Ervin Laszlo began by emphasizing the unprecedented speed with which change is taking place today. Some spheres have already globalized: eg science, the media, finance, and business (to an extent). However, politicians and governments lag behind. Laszlo believes that globalization is inevitable since the present order is non-sustainable. We should not shrink from facing unpredictability (of the forms described by Blenk) but we should aim to make decisions so as to 'enhance the probability of positive outcomes'. Reform must take place in media and business (which currently emphasizes the sensational, the short-term), and the 'unrecognized value' of religion – torn by internal strife – ought to be recognized. He mentioned the Bahá'í Faith as having an answer to the need for 'unity in diversity'.

In the discussion, the audience focused on how to develop in young people an ability to think creatively in terms of complex processes, in a world context in which the media and fundamentalism serve to oversimplify and sensationalize in ways that provoke violent conflict.

THE EVOLUTIONARY CONTEXT OF THE TRANSITION

Ilya Prigogine began by indicating that a small handful of scientists have changed our outlook more quickly and more extensively than have religious leaders. However, the classical world picture, that truth is timeless and laws universal, has been shattered by recent discoveries in quantum mechanics and non-equilibrium physics. Recognition of the factors of time and the position of the observer have led to a realization of the inherent instability and unpredictability of nature.

The chaotic quality of nature may be thought of as having a positive dimension. It represents how life forms 'explore possibilities', like the brain itself which, when too regular in functioning, approaches states identified as brain disease. A veritable 'second Copernican revolution' has occurred due to our understanding of the dynamics and implications of irregularity. The growing sense of nature resembles views of the ancient Indians and Chinese, views that suggest both a fundamental unity between the functioning of human beings and nature, and the inseparability of the processes of human research and the processes of environmental change.

In conclusion, Prigogine argued that the emerging scientific world-view that emphasizes both complexity and interaction and the growth of identity within the process of differentiation (self-organization), is much more congenial to egalitarian democracy than the classical world-view of science, which legitimated and provoked hierarchy and domination (of man over nature, one culture over another, etc).

In the discussion Laszlo raised questions concerning refinement of the theories presented, whereas Bushrui started a debate on the role of morality in scientific research. Prigogine responded to both, emphasizing that citizens together with scientists must shape the ethics of research and application.

Robert Artigiani began by indicating that history teaches us two things: 1) that we tend to look to the past for Utopian blueprints but these have always gone wrong; and 2) those who fail in their endeavours tend to blame the world, not their theory. Nazism and Stalinism were mentioned as examples. He argued that we cannot predict the future much less impose our vision upon society. Rather, we should focus on 'rules' instead of presumed 'maps' of the future. He used the US constitution as an example.

Pentti Malaska presented a graphic model of society in harmony. Harmony occurs when optimal 'cross-catalytic interaction' takes place between six basic dimensions: social, economic, spiritual, political, cultural, and material. When one of the dimensions is blocked or dominated by another, then society may be said to be out of balance. Examples given were Eastern Europe (political domination) and Iran (spiritual domination).

Miriam Campanella spoke of problems associated with globalization, such as the threat it poses to local values and cultures, and the vulnerability that comes with interdependence. Some of the traps we need to avoid in analysing the transition include that of treating systems in isolation and limiting ourselves to short-term perspectives.

Day Two
Wednesday 5 September 1990

THE GOVERNANCE OF THE TRANSITION: THE ROLE OF THE
PUBLIC SECTOR

Federico Mayor argued that 'freedom is the gate to all other principles of human dignity'. However, during the past two centuries some societies have overemphasized freedom while others have overemphasized equity; and both have forgotten the importance of solidarity. Speaking of UNESCO'S efforts to preserve famous monuments, Mayor argued that the uniqueness of each individual was the most important monument to preserve. However, the many world crises – eg environment, poverty, and political process – prevent achievement of human development. Scholars must overcome the 'introversion' of specialization, and citizens must overcome 'compassion fatigue' to actively promote viable solutions to these crises.

In the discussion Henri Janne said that we need to be careful to determine the minimum scale of action to be really effective in development efforts. Success or failure tends to have a domino effect. A lively discussion ensued concerning the impact of television on behaviour in diverse parts of the world, with Mayor arguing for complete freedom and others pointing out the drawbacks of such freedom in the West.

Bohdan Hawrylyshyn discussed the problem of transition in eastern bloc societies. Some will have to pass through a stage of nationalism before becoming 'globally conscious'. He explained general models of political order and economic system contrasting Soviet-style society with western societies, indicating how models could be constructed that avoided the extremes. He advocated a conflict-free, unregulated market system featuring power-sharing and direct democracy.

In the discussion Bushrui sounded a note of caution that even the best models cannot succeed if the human being is faulty. Hawrylyshyn agreed but indicated the danger of narcissism if the social dimension is neglected in favour of individual development.

Volodymyr Vassilenko described the current situation in the former Soviet republics. He reminded us that the USSR was not a single nation, but rather a federation of fifteen sovereign states each of which had the constitutional power to enter into relations with foreign countries and take part in international organizations. They were oppressed by a centralized bureaucratic structure that ignored these rights and overtaxed the states. He argued that, for years, western countries had ignored this situation in order to pursue their own security interests. The republics now want free and direct collaboration with European countries.

In the discussion, Singh voiced concern about the possible fragmentation of India and China inspired by the Soviet example, and raised the issue of Islamic fundamentalism. Hawrylyshyn indicated that the problem in the USSR is not ethnic as proved by the fact that one fifth of the population of the Ukraine is Russian. Vassilenko added that the Russians in the Ukraine supported Ukrainian independence.

Adamou Ndam Njoya argued that we must give more importance to human beings. At each level of human society we find the expressions of both generosity and selfishness. Njoya traced the development of these characteristics in the international sphere during the twentieth century. One obstacle to international generosity has to do with the nationalist fashion in which diplomats are trained. He advocated a multinational centre to train diplomats for global society.

In the discussion Gérard de Puymège advocated use of the concept of 'person', which emphasizes the relationship between the individual and the collectivity.

Hawrylyshyn stressed that in our efforts to globalize we should not forget that small countries are more easily managed. Let us not be swayed merely by economists' arguments about the advantages of large-scale operations.

Mayor urged us to strive for 'perpetual rebellion'. Otherwise sustainable evolution may not be achieved. The twentieth century has taught us 'the price of war'. But now we must face up to 'the price of peace'. To do this, however, our 'inner Berlin wall' must fall – that is, our tendency to maintain that it is the other individual or group that must change, not us. In our efforts to foster human development on a global scale we must also reach the multitudes who are currently 'outside of development and democracy'.

Day Three
Thursday 6 September 1990

THE MANAGEMENT OF THE TRANSITION: THE ROLE OF THE
PRIVATE SECTOR

Bertrand Schneider began by listing over two dozen major changes in the world since 1972, such as the diminishing of the role of the two superpowers, the flourishing of fundamentalism, the unfulfilled aspirations of the 'so-called Third World', AIDS, and European unity. He emphasized that all of these changes are interconnected. Schneider then focused on the disturbing factors associated with the 'greenhouse effect', 'underdevelopment and population' (world population is likely to double between the year 2000 and 2500), and the 'degradation of the soil'. He argued that education must overcome apathy, double standards, and fanaticism if we are to survive the severe stresses that face us.

Dieter Tober began by showing the many ways in which the dream of one world is gradually being realized by political and economic initiatives. He traced out the origins of globalization, eg in deregulation, denationalization of state-owned enterprises, and the new capacities of technology and transport. Nevertheless, a major obstacle exists in North–South trade and labour relations, which are connected with the massive debts of the poorer nations. There has also been a trend toward a 'multi-polar world' (East Asia, Western Europe and North America), the dynamics of which tend to hamper the process of globalization.

Martin Lees concentrated on the more 'speculative' aspects of economic change. He stressed that our difficulty in being able to foresee and manage the future is due to:

(a) The inadequacy in our legalistic way of thinking;
(b) The assumption that we are in transition to a particular end point;
(c) The assumption that the world is currently being managed at all; and
(d) The assumption that development must proceed through either the public or private sectors.

We must face the fact that the world is very volatile, complex, and perhaps even out of control. He went on to offer prognoses for the economies of the United States (which has become the world's largest debtor nation), Japan (which will have accumulated $500 billion to $1 trillion in assets by 1995), the EEC (which represents good foresight), and the former socialist countries (all of which must achieve a better balance between their public and private sectors). Overall, the private sector has demonstrated greater responsiveness to change (than the public sector) but international management of the world economy is needed, and this will require general public support.

Day Four
Friday 7 September 1990

THE ROLE OF SCIENCE AND TECHNOLOGY IN THE TRANSITION

Sam Nilsson began by expressing concern that the science and technology sector has been losing touch with humanism. The former should be regarded 'as a tool, not an end'. The greatest problem business leaders are facing today is the 'management of technology'. He spoke of dimensions of global problems such as the greenhouse effect ('heat death' it should be called, he said), desertification, and the high cost of the public sector. He argued that socialism has failed, not because of its value system, but rather because the 'tribal altruism' it presupposes cannot thrive in large-scale mass society. Humanism needs to become the 'leading value system', and inefficient intergovernmental aid programmes ought to continue being replaced by more direct aid between sister-villages or churches.

Ian Angell feared that information technology (IT), itself in transition, is more likely to complicate than to ease the transition to global society. He pointed to the risk of 'electronic slavery', and of accidents due to a paucity of understanding and control, like the magic wand in the hands of a sorcerer's apprentice. Designed to replace manpower, IT is ironically dependent on people, its operators, who must accordingly be of a high calibre.

Carl-Göran Heden described the consequences of current resource and energy use policies, stressing the need for alternative sources. For instance, for every tree planted we are cutting down ten – coal use is likely to go up forty per cent by the year 2000. Instead of coal and oil we need to use non-polluting, regenerative resources. Examples are being produced through bio-technological engineering. He advocated that we take seriously the UN's 'human development index' when costing out energy alternatives.

In the discussion, Artigiani stressed that we must find enduring values that enrich change. Singh indicated that he felt Angell had been too critical of technology. In India, for instance, we can now forecast monsoons and take precautions against them. The key is to use technology wisely.

Njoya emphasized that we need to avoid ruining cultures through the introduction of technologies. Rather, the latter need to be applied in ways that foster cultural and spiritual development. He cited the problem of how easily money and brains get drained away from the developing countries.

Janne agreed with Nilsson that the ethical dimension of technological change is the main problem. But, said Janne, 'Who chooses the goals? Who uses the results? Who makes the profits? What are the political economic powers manipulating scientific and technological policies?'

Laszlo addressed the larger conception of transition, emphasizing that one dimension is not the secret, rather all dimensions are important. Planners need a 'grasp of the situation' as a whole, and to tie together many approaches.

THE ROLE OF CULTURE IN THE TRANSITION

Henri Janne began by defining the term 'culture', which is the realization of the spiritual, material, intellectual, and psychological dimensions of humanity. He spoke of the concepts of identity and cultural imperialism. European culture is composed of the rationality of the Romans, Christianity (from the fourth century on), humanism (from the sixteenth century), Enlightenment liberalism (from the seventeenth century). Attempts were made to universalize this culture, but the means (colonialism) were often at the expense of basic European values (eg equality, liberty). Though improvements were made in conquered countries, racial prejudice also was a result.

After all, European culture is not truly universal. It lacks the oriental wisdoms, and the practices of mastery over body and spirit. It lacks the African norms of community in daily life, which ensure social continuity. Janne predicts a dialectical tension between two cultural forces in the world: one leading to universalism, the other to localism (in the form of fundamentalism or nationalism).

Iván Vitanyi began by describing the dynamics of the post-fifteenth-century capitalist world system (Wallerstein) and the current role of modern communications. Culture has manifested a contradictory role: it conserves yet transforms, retards yet adapts. But in capitalist society we see the emergence of mass, 'pragmatic culture' accompanied by a large entertainment industry. European high culture (eg as characterized by Janne) belongs only to a small elite, whereas the masses absorb only fragments of ideals and practices, little of which is autochthonous, all of which is poorly integrated. The result is low efficiency. He concluded by pointing out the glaring contradiction between the value of equality in the West and the reality of underdevelopment on the periphery, to the point that there appears to be a 'system of inequality'. An 'emancipatory global culture' is needed, free from political-economic domination.

In the discussion, De Puymège attributed the modern dynamism of Europe to its commitment to the truth, liberty, and progress. All of the great movements in the field of art have been spawned by the nations of Europe, a reflection of the European character of the culture.

Sara Miller-McCune argued that De Puymège's perspective was Eurocentric, that he ignored the vast contributions of ancient civilizations. Lily Ayman said that we should not talk of regional cultures, rather we should focus on universals, world civilizations. Berenice Bleedorn quoted an unnamed author: 'Unity without diversity is uniformity . . . justice is when there is creative tension between unity and diversity.' José Vidal-Beneyto returned to De Puymège's argument claiming that in the West 'subjectivity' has a character different from that in China or Africa.

De Puymège, responding to criticism, indicated that by defining the features of European culture he did not mean 'to cast scorn' on other civilizations. He described his previous professional activities, which are consistent with an egalitarian attitude.

Heden suggested that world culture might be organized along the lines of the human body which is greatly decentralized.

James Malarkey, reflecting on the emotionally charged exchanges surrounding De Puymège's first intervention, pointed out that today we are experiencing an acute contradiction. As the cultures of the world contact one another in order to collaborate, much more patience is needed than ordinarily presumed. Yet, given the overwhelming speed of change, we have virtually no time for patience. What we need is a 'science of patience' which can help us understand others' perspectives and avoid potential disaster.

Laszlo introduced the next two speakers who, with Vitanyi, were part of a project called EUROCIRCON, the aim of which is to study the prospects of European unity and the implications for eventual world unity.

Mária Sági described her research in Hungary on national, regional and global identity. Among her discoveries were that a broader sense of identity tends to be found among those in the liberal arts as contrasted with those who work in the hard sciences. Those who have a strong Hungarian identity often also possess global identity. Her research indicates that people can become more inclusive without sacrificing more local loyalties. Responding to Malarkey's earlier intervention concerning the need for patience, she suggested that people whose own selves are more diversified or differentiated possess a greater ability to embrace the diversity of other peoples and cultures.

Sonya Licht began by arguing that Europe will have a role in the transition only if it can preserve multicultural diversity and integrate democracy without the imposition from above of any one ideology. Solutions must come from below. Immigrants must be better integrated into European societies, since they 'bring the benefits of cross-cultural contact' to those Europeans who cannot travel. She remarked on the tendency of easterners to happily identify themselves as Europeans while to westerners the identity was uninspiring. The main hope for Eastern Europe lies in its ability to think of itself in global terms, rather than limiting its self-conception to 'western' or 'European' identity. Yet to achieve this would seem to involve a new period of nationalism. She went on to discuss problems concerning mutual perceptions between East Europeans and Third World peoples.

Allan Williams addressed the issue of tourism in relation to economic change and global education. Only in the nineteenth century did the middle class begin to engage in tourism. By 1950 there were twenty-five million tourists; 160 million in 1970; and 350 million in 1990. For westerners tourism has come to be seen as an 'entitlement'. Most of it, however, is confined to the 'pleasure periphery' (to regions of sun or snow); and tourists tend to follow paths established for them by the media and airline companies, often to former colonies. Aside from the growth of a small percentage of tours with an educational focus, most tours involve increasingly limited contact with natives. Yet, the potential for education remains great.

In the discussion Mildred Mottahedeh indicated that Williams omitted to mention business travellers and student exchange programmes. Williams responded that eighty per cent of tourism is of the holiday variety.

Charles Nolley addressed the larger issue of education, indicating that the Sioux Indians have a greater sense of world citizenship than their anglo neighbours. His research indicated that they also know more world geography. He added that we may not be able to predict where the 'centre' will be, as global society emerges. It may not be in Europe or in the US.

Bleedorn referred to astronaut Edgar Mitchell's vision of the world as a whole, then to her own such epiphany at International University. She quoted an Indian woman who said that 'God is a sphere, the centre of which is everywhere, the perimeter nowhere'.

Helen Muller raised the question of the McDonalds franchise in the global perspective. Licht indicated that there were always two long lines in one quarter of Moscow, one in front of an office of publications, the other in front of McDonalds. Muller added that the special training workers receive at McDonald's may eventually boost the quality of customer relations.

Heden commented that medical schools are now sending students to diverse countries for training. Experiential tours are also available, eg to Antarctica or the Amazon. Williams added that rucksack travel is also important.

Day Five
Saturday 8 September 1990

NEW VISION, NEW VALUES: THE EMERGENCE OF A
NEW WORLD ORDER

Dorothy Nelson opened the session by arguing that a major feature of a new world order involves justice as a goal of universal education. Preconditions of justice include the elimination of prejudice, reduction of the inequalities in wealth, greater equality between men and women (without eliminating their distinctiveness), and the recognition of the progressive character of both religious and scientific truth.

John Huddleston began by defining vision, and noting that prophets have been the greatest inspirers of civilization. However, over time their messages have often become deformed by corrupted institutions. Recently, socialist systems have shown themselves to suffer from inefficiency and lack of incentive despite the noble aspirations of egalitarianism and co-operation. Although democratic capitalism may seem to have won out, it is unsustainable, and it possesses a 'hollow core'. He enumerated some of the disturbing trends in the US that betray a lack of long-term vision: eg electioneering, parochialism, family disintegration, rampant take-overs ignoring the well-being of employees, the decline of savings rates commensurate with national debt achieving an all-time high. He advocated a return to the 'essence' of our religious heritage which can instil in us a sense of the sacred interdependence of life and a realization that mankind is one family and should be regarded as such.

Ingo Hofmann began by indicating the difficulty of establishing a correlation between the information explosion and religion. Studies show that German adults remember only twenty-five per cent of the news viewed on television, and sixty-five per cent of this percentage they remember incorrectly. Nevertheless, the media are taking over the integration functions formerly provided by religion. But the advances in scientific understanding made possible by new technology are limited in capacity, since quantities of information are less effective as a unifying force than the sacred word, divine revelation. The difficulty with religious literature is that it tends to mix information with metaphysics. He went on to show how *The Seven Valleys* of Bahá'u'lláh reconciles both in metaphysical form, as the seeker passes through the valleys of search, love, knowledge, and unity to the valleys of contentment, wonderment, and true poverty. He concluded by explaining how in the process of Bahá'í 'consultation', science and religion coalesce leading to informed, unified action.

Janet Khan provided two case studies of social transformation sponsored by the Bahá'í International Community. The theory of 'evolutionary education' is being used to help struggling communities establish a powerful vision for their future, and to elect councils to organize their strategies for change. In Panama, Indians are encouraged to focus on their potential for enlightening and rehabilitating humanity. The process of consultation carries them from vision to actualization. Along the way old traditions are revived which are conducive to progress (eg consensus, united action) while customs that obstruct progress decline (eg the subordination of women). Radio is used to transmit the new vision, sometimes using traditional forms of legend and folklore. A striking educational feature of a similar project in Columbia involves the organization of courses of study conceived as 'acts of service in the community'.

In the discussion Emma Broisman expressed disappointment that religion was emphasized in a session on 'new world order'. Religion has been historically divisive; and she contended we are on the brink of a Third World war due to religion. Her experience in the field of development has led her to conclude that it should involve providing technical assistance without including spirituality. Hofmann responded by saying that reason and science have also been divisive. Religion is, indeed, counterproductive if it is exclusive and dogmatic.

Singh spoke of the existence of religious unity, the universal ideas that thread through all religions. The 'Perennial Philosophy' is still pertinent. If we ignore this civilizing current of religion we leave it to the fanatics who are divisive. He mentioned the unifying Dialogue planned by the Temple of Understanding.

Elaine McCreary spoke of the widespread character of spirituality. In her Graduate School of Social Development the goal is to foster 'mutual transformation' between cultures in contact, including spirituality. Years of failure trying merely to adapt western innovations to local contexts have pointed up the futility of trying to 'imperialize'.

Njoya, responding to Broisman's initial intervention, indicated that such questions are always raised about religion. One example of efforts under way to get beyond dogma include the World Conference of Religions for Peace (sponsored by UNICEF).

Kathleen Raine recalled the words of Blake in the eighteenth century that all religions are one. The differences are cultural, not intrinsic, she added. There are two dangers to avoid: religion being viewed in merely its organizational aspect; and the blending of all religions into a 'grey soup'.

Huddleston spoke of the widespread prejudice against religion in Europe. A new system cannot be improved from above; it would have to come from the people. Lord Thurlow said that we all share spirituality, though not religion, and we tend to neglect the development of the former. In eastern civilization there are examples of how spiritual development can be found – eg yoga. Mahmud Samandari cautioned us that the majority of the world is guided by spiritual values, therefore it would be imperialistic of the West to impose secularization.

Silvia Staub-Bernasconi asked Hofmann to explain the idea that in consultation it is better to be wrong and united than right and disunited. Hofmann responded that this approach is not to be applied to empirical or scientific problems; but, rather, to matters of judgement. Historically, societies have suffered the tyranny of individual decision-makers. The method of consultation is designed to cultivate group consensus. Staub-Bernasconi then asked Huddleston if he had applied his principles to his own workplace. Huddleston said he had started an informal ethics group a few years ago. The composition has grown and now includes the Managing Director and the President of the World Bank.

Arthur Zobrist indicated that there had not been enough dialogue at the Dialogue. Instead, there had been a lot of 'scientific exhibitionism'. Huschmand Sabet suggested that before us is a big vision of everlasting peace. We must be modest, open, and learn from other cultures. Mikhail Kopylov expressed dismay that none of the panelists had proposed solutions to the worldwide ecological crisis. We need institutions that can help solve these problems. Miller-McCune indicated that she was disturbed by Huddleston's somewhat negative image of the United States. Perhaps the media gives us an inadequate image of reality. Huddleston commented that the United States is now the leading model of capitalistic democracy, which many previously socialist countries are now looking to emulate. To balance the tendency to romanticize, the weakness of the US example must be pointed out. But the America of Jefferson, Lincoln, Roosevelt, and Wilson can be built upon.

Bushrui, responding to Zobrist, indicated that the Dialogue was a first experiment that we must aim to improve upon. 'Let us go forth united in love and solidarity'.

HUMANISTIC PERSPECTIVES OF THE TRADITION: THE ROLE OF PRACTICAL ETHICS

Francis Warner portrayed historical examples of practical ethics in five contexts: the Athens of Pericles, Rome, Byzantium, Florence, and Romantic Europe. Among the Romans, unlike the Greeks, concern over hierarchy eclipsed commitment to equality. The Roman ethic was to impose its civilization, then offer peace. But 'the ancient world lacked a concept to complete the reckoning between ideas and persons' – that is, the concept of 'forgiveness'. After paganism there was a shift in ethics. After the Middle Ages life came to be seen either through 'persons' (the Renaissance) or through ideas (eg Marxism), against which Romanticism was a reaction. Warner remarked on the pattern of great plagues occurring after periods of great injustice, and gave historical examples.

Kathleen Raine argued that science cannot teach us the 'language of the soul'. We must look to poetry to understand humanity and the powers beyond the measurable material world. If we do not reconnect with the lost 'sources' of spirituality, then culture will remain only 'cosmic'. She quoted Yeats, 'Things fall apart / The centre cannot hold . . .', suggesting that we can only recover 'the centre' through the arts of the imagination. In so doing, we will realize that the allure of material things when shared diminishes. When the imaginative arts are shared each receives the whole undiminished.

Though each tribe or nation may have its own imaginative identity, the products of each can belong to humanity as a whole. The perennial wisdom can alone bring about unity, and this unity is 'a shared vision of eternity'.

Suheil Bushrui quoted Shelley's statement that 'poets are the unacknowledged legislators of the world'. He gave examples, emphasizing the achievement of Goethe, whose *East-West Diwan* embodied a creative unity between East and West through his translation of the Persian poet, Hafez. Bushrui argued that science had come to replace the tyrannic schoolmen of Europe; and the poets have continued to caution us against the hubris of science. He spoke briefly of Yeats's foresight – ignored by the politicians, and then read the poet's 'Second Coming' and W. H. Auden's 'In Memory of W. B. Yeats', adding suggestive comments.

In the discussion Heden remarked that the pessimism about science was not really justified. Artigiani followed by referring to the radical revolutions in science during the twentieth century. It is no longer a monolithic entity; and now as much emphasis is on relationships as on material substance.

Bleedorn, responding to Kopylov's earlier intervention, suggested that the concept of 'global brain' implies an ethical position regarding the environment.

Raine clarified her reservation about science. What she questions are the assumptions that the material order is all there is, and that the observed is more real than the observer. Singh indicated that scientific materialism has actually been collapsing. Artigiani added that the bankruptcy of materialism was presaged as far back as 1927 by Eddington. Heisenberg's demonstration of the 'uncertainty' principle was of decisive importance.

Polakoff, responding to an earlier comment by Muller, indicated that business schools are offering much greater attention to ethics than was formerly the case, 'in every functional area'. Janne indicated that scientists are concerned with ethics and values, but science is manipulated by military, political and economic interests.

Hofmann said that the success of science has grown out of an ability to exploit specific principles to the ultimate. However, there is a danger of losing sight of wholeness. Religion is a power that teaches love; and this force must be combined with science.

Mottahedeh suggested that what we need is 'an international ethical code'. Bushrui, referring to Schiller's On the Aesthetic Education of Man, advocated that ethics must begin with the individual.

Heden mentioned that 150 countries have signed the treaty on chemical weapons. But politicians ignore such treaties when they want to use such weapons.

Karan Singh began the final speech of the Dialogue by speaking of major changes of the twentieth century. If science and technology are used with wisdom, peace will be the dividend. Global sensitivity is needed, but so is the awareness of our deepest selves. The 'inner quest' is becoming increasingly significant. He recounted an ancient Indian myth which ended with Shiva shooting an arrow through three walls to kill the terrifying demon. From the demon's death, Atman emerged. The lesson is that, despite the boundaries of our apparent selves, there is an immortal self in all beings, and this self – if we help it to emerge – is the base of ethics. We must nurture this higher consciousness. Singh concluded the Dialogue with an invocation to the mother Earth goddess, imagined seated on a white lotus, holding a lotus flower in each hand (symbolizing the unfolding of each Atman) . . .